CARAVANSARY

By Richard de Combray

CARAVANSARY
VENICE, FRAIL BARRIER
ATTITUDES ESPAGNOLES,
in collaboration with Michel Del Castillo

Richard de Combray

CARAVANSARY

Alone in Moslem Places

Published by Doubleday & Company, Inc.   Garden City, New York   1978

Library of Congress Cataloging in Publication Data

Combray, Richard de.
Caravansary: Alone in Moslem Places

1. Moslem countries—Description and travel.
2. Combray, Richard de.   I.   Title.
DS36.65.C65   916'.04'3
ISBN: 0-385-11206-8
Library of Congress Catalog Card Number 77–82621

CONTENTS

For Jean, Mischa and for Miles
and our Mediterranean of then.

The author wishes to thank these three close friends for their part in this book: Alex and Pepe Karmel, who shared many North African adventures, and Steven Woodward Naifeh, who, along with his family, made it possible to discover the Persian Gulf. The New York Society Library with its collective goodwill simplified the mechanics of research on Seventy-ninth Street C.S., D.M.G. and R.G.M.S. were responsible for certain photographic details; and Michele Tempesta's spirited guidance prevailed throughout.

Wherever I walked, the ground fell away under me and the stars fell from the sky.

—Isak Dinesen, Out of Africa

CARAVANSARY

Caravansary: (Persian kārwānsarāï; kārwān, *caravan* + sarāï, *palace, mansion, inn). In the Orient, a sort of inn with a large central court, where caravans stop for the night.*

A book about travel is in many ways a book about solitude. No matter how many adventures along the way, the traveler must inevitably return to a series of bleak, transient rooms. There, his only familiar companions are the belongings brought in his own baggage, the only warmth comes from the thin blanket covering the bed. But it is unwise to mention the bed, mute, its miserable history sealed inside its mattress. He is alone.

He has been a collector of swift views, of people caught mid-life, blurred between one step and another. Narrowing himself down to make room for them he risks, in these encounters, forgetting who he is. No one has really asked him anyway. It is he who asks, he who listens. Longing to tell some tale of his own, he returns to those transient rooms to stare at the walls; gradually (such is the power of solitude) they assume a different aspect. Now he finds himself in a phantom stopping-place, a caravansary of shapes and colors that have passed his way and left, taking even their shadows with them. Only then can he begin his story.

Chapter One

FEZ, TANGIER, TIME
AND A TRAIN

You are pulled downwards in Fez: down, down, whirlpooling through narrow alleys, circling mean little squares where one tree stands, down again past high doorways, higher walls; sudden monumental courtyards hide behind insignificant archways flanked by false-teeth shops and dusty bolts of cotton; you skid on some substance, right yourself as you descend, lurching now into an alley that ends with an indecipherable stone plaque on a blank wall, the hand of Fatima chalked in above it. Where does the eddy finally flow? Where is there a flat place at the bottom, a base on which this tortuous city revolves? It is to remain a mystery, for now you have begun again to climb. Alleys wobble off on all sides of you, bent spokes slanting upwards. Robed figures disappear around corners just as you sight them along the worn, paved cobblestones. The emptiness above pulls you back up, now with some hope, now towards the green hills surrounding the city. A mule comes towards you, filled bags flanking its saddle. Given the narrowness of the alleys, how can it pass? You press yourself against a wall. A child leans out from someplace: "*Ça va?*" he asks.

"*Oui, ça va,*" you say, noting that the small opening from which he emerged contains in it four more children and a man, all of them working on cedarwood, turning it with fingers and toes into handles for skewering lambs. *Shishkabob,* they say in unison. Just beyond, another child holds in his uplifted fists two spools of bright thread gradually unwinding themselves into a loom worked by a man seated in another doorway. They have nothing to sell. They do not look up as you pass.

Radio sounds emerge from inside these walls. Songs—long, low laments—fade away and return again from a surface nearby, the same phantasmal station filling the city streets and alleys. The sounds are elastic strands of melancholy. The smells are strewn and blown about. You barely have time to ponder what spice is in the air when a blast of something so putrid and decomposing sends you staggering away in an attempt to avoid it. The flies circle around you, around the meager, neat food displays, lighting on the sugary things, the meats, the whole calves' heads still dripping from their hooks. Someone with a glaucous eye sits in a doorway and the flies crawl on him, dotting his eyelids. He remains there unflinching. You climb, you climb, searching overhead for the sky, but it is latticed from view.

Such is the imperial city of Fez. Once the teachings of Aristotle were preserved here when Europe had lost the track of its history. Scholars strolled through the gardens of the madersas, the reflecting pools and fountains and fruit trees their shimmering companions. The town was walled; each quarter could be locked. Still there are few windows. Everything is hidden. Each street turns in on itself, each house is contained within its own parapet, each family is separate from the rest, each individual is at the will of Allah.

During the winter the scent of wood fires fills the air. It rains, the city is cold, a subterranean dankness hugs the heavy, undecorated walls and the streets are still. I visited Fez one winter staying in a dilapidated hotel perched high above the city, aloof. A massive gate in front of it clanged shut in the evenings. On my last day there I went out alone, realizing after a while that I had gotten lost in the alleys: Fez was Venice, without the canals, formed into a funnel. Certain sights seemed familiar, and in gratitude I approached them only to discover my mistake. I was fated to lose my way in the Arab world. I realize this only now as I collect these memories.

The streets coaxed me on, each corner promising some sign of recognition. By now I was in some part of town that I no longer knew. I asked the people I passed for directions and they barely stopped, with puzzled expressions, before hurrying on, ghost figures disappearing into doorways, their long robes illuminating them in the mist. I turned the corner of a narrow alley and walked into a large burlap sack. It moved, pulsing with some incomprehensible life.

In my confusion, I began to mutter an apology. Then I saw an ancient man concealed in a doorway, lost in the folds of his djellaba. He held up his hand to stop me from leaving. Then, with very slow, deliberate steps, he approached. His heavy eyelids slid down over his eyes and he smiled a hooded smile. I stood rooted to the spot, mid-turn, with something resembling terror. Death must approach in such a way. "*Rkhess*" cheap, he said, and he pointed to the sack. Then he brought his weathered hand towards his stomach, making a crabbed circle with it in the air. He licked his lips, reaching quickly into the sack to withdraw a crazed, fluttering bird. "*Makla*" food, he said, holding it fast by its legs. Then he snapped the neck of the bird.

The sky had darkened. The bird hung from his hand, its quick eyes still open. Bare patches covered its thin breast. Like a half-open fan, its wing

shielded its dangling legs.

"I'll buy them," I heard myself say, putting money into his hand. The sack next to him continued to move with small spasms. Reopening it cautiously, he gathered up one bird, then another, meticulously packing them into my camera bag. He stopped, mumbling to himself as he made his calculations, and then reached into his sack. When there was no more room, I took the birds in my hands, where they hung from my fingers. I said the name of my hotel, he pointed, and I began to run in that direction. It was now raining hard. Water poured through the lattices above the streets. The birds swayed, suspended between my fingers, their wings no longer flapping. Finally, I came to a clearing and saw the hotel and its garden above me. When I got to the garden I let the birds loose. Some of them fell to the ground, but then they lifted into the air, each one taking a separate path, disappearing over the green tiled rooftops.

I brushed against the Arab world the first time, in a dream. I must have been eleven or twelve, and in the dream I wore a turban. Running along a deserted beach I discovered a bottle, corked, which I picked up suspiciously and opened. Immediately the compressed jinni it contained emerged in a rush to cover the sky.

"Come with me," it said in gratitude from some great height, "and I will show you the world."

Golden domes and minarets arose in the distance. I reached up towards the jinni in fear and excitement. And as I tried to attach myself to this vast, miraculous transportation, a wholly new warmth rocked me out of my dream and back into my childhood room in a dazzlement.

When I was twenty I walked for the first time along the shores of North Africa in Tangier. Two things happened then. The first was that I fell in love with the girl who was traveling with and who would eventually marry my closest friend. They were sitting at a café table, at dusk, hands entwined, on the narrow terrace fronting their hotel. It was a small shabby-romantic building at the entrance to the kasbah. She looked up, annoyed at the interruption. I had surprised them. I was supposed to have been in Spain. Her Tartar eyes studied me with some amusement as we were introduced. Her face, at that moment, still haunts me, for I see it in the particular mauve light that bathes Morocco just before sunset. Then the three of us drifted down the dark alleys together, excited to be in a kasbah. We drank mint tea high on the ramparts overlooking the sea and smoked kif in my fancy hotel room, for I was traveling in great style at the time. It was to be my last such trip for a long while.

On the balcony outside the room we danced to music drifting up from the gardens below where couples more stately and grownup than we swayed primly to ". . . a sigh is just a sigh," as the lights of Spain flickered way off in the distance. We thought in some irrational way that we three would never be separated, that we would grow old together always near the richness of the Mediterranean. We did not know that we were never to see the Mediterranean together again. We could not know then that she would die in her thirtieth year in New York on a night without stars. Only good things were ahead of us, it seemed. Such is the power of the Mediterranean.

In addition to falling in love, I felt (at twenty) that I had discovered another planet, the *lodestar east*, that had lured such heroes of mine as Burton and Lawrence. I met a young Moroccan, Abdultif, who offered to find me a small apartment so that I could stay in Tangier until some vaporous time in the future. Time was then without clear margins, and the Arab world was a suitable atmosphere to support this habit. The house would overlook the harbor, he promised, from the walls of the kasbah, pressed against the other whitewashed houses on the rise of the hill. I was tempted, of course. But I was never to see the place. Instead I went back to Paris to a hotel on the Quai Voltaire.

Tangier is easy. Perhaps it is too easy, too cheerful, too much a part of southern Europe. Everywhere there is a hand extended, a smile, a salute. No matter if the gesture comes out incorrectly. VISIT SUNNY TANGIER THE CITY THAT SLOPS DOWN TO THE SEA, it says on a travel poster. LA BANQUE POPULAIRE DU NORD BIDS YOU A VERY WORM WELCOME! is written across the bright-orange friendly brochure put out by the Bureau of Tourism. You realize by the general absence of their influence how the French have crippled affability in the rest of North Africa. The interdictions and suspicions they practice at home and have imported to their colonies found ready acceptance among the Arabs, who had those tendencies anyway. But Tangier has hugged close to Spain—its south, that is. "Just a kiss away from Spain," says Royal Air Maroc. A real-life travelogue.

There is the *paseo* at the end of the day. The main street is blocked off at seven so that everyone can walk back and forth with no cars to spoil their fun. A child cartwheels by in front of the Café de Paris dressed in a scarlet satin acrobat's costume his mother made. He lands on his feet, arms outstretched for the spare change. Someone has a monkey on a chain holding out a cup and it walks with urgency to each café table as though searching for a relative. Parents push baby carriages never seen in most of the Arab world—and these are as elaborate as Bentleys—rolling past turbaned elders leaning against biblical staves, nodding gravely to each other. Boys stroll by in twos, sleeked up in tight clothes looking for adventure. Pubescent girls gather like swallows on the line, as heavily made up as Gypsies. And if some of them are veiled they are no less interested in or interesting to the general air of provocation.

Spanish women made up to the nines, traveling in threes and fours, having brought up children and buried husbands, are now down on vacation

from Madrid stuffed into dresses that might have once been fashionable. They are durable ladies. They are wrinkled and brave. Their fierce noses have sought after and inhaled everything from Andalusian orange blossoms in April through the smoke of civil war and they have survived. Up come their fans. With a flick of their wrists they become fluttering girls once again without missing a beat in their proud promenade.

Tailors and shirtmakers have their shops open until ten or eleven. The Spanish barbers keep going past midnight, calling themselves names like Haut Coiffeur de Paris. There is a lineup of customers slouched on the high-backed chairs. Once fussed-over locks gather in glossy drifts on the linoleum floor, spinning round like autumn leaves when the door opens for another client. There are fast cars accelerating through the boulevards in the new town. Girls perch next to the drivers sidewise, the way they've seen it at the movies. And in the old town bicycles can barely get through the narrow alleys. The merchants slowly close up and carefully lock stalls no larger than Park Avenue closets, curling up in their robes to sleep next to the thick walls, the stones whitewashed and whitewashed again through the years. It is an old city, older than old. The centuries have picked it clean.

There is no sense in Tangier of its dense history, no architectural cheek-by-jowl index of the centuries it has endured. It looks as though a film company could have put it together in a week to crown a hill overlooking the sea. When Caesar created Africa Nova in 45 B.C., Carthage occupied this land. Rome gave it the name of Tingis, and it remained Roman for almost seven centuries, roughly the span of time between Christ and Mohammed. In the Moslem expansion, the Arabs would conquer territory as far as Samarkand and the Punjab. Across the Straits of Gibraltar they claimed Spain, entering France at the Pyrenees in 717. For seven centuries Tangier remained under the restless domination of Arab and Turkish rule. Then it was occupied by the Portuguese at the time the world was certified as round.

Kings, Califs, Sultans reigned. The Spanish gave Tangier to England as part of a dowry for Charles II. In the eighteenth century it was isolated from the rest of the land by Moulay Ismail, founder of Meknes, who sent all his Christian ambassadors there. The particular aloof nature of the city remained. In this century, when the French and Spanish carved Morocco into protectorates—the French getting the best part, of course—it was retained as an international territory. In the 1950's, on the streets leading down to the kasbah, itinerant money changers carried small blackboards chalked in with the latest exchanges. Foreign currency was hawked as casually as Parker pens. It was the extreme edge of the Eastern world and anyone could visit by taking the ferry south from Spain. When Morocco was united in 1956, the character of the city was too well established to change much. Now it is more of an extended carnival than ever.

Money has come to the *ville nouvelle*. There is neon, there are television aerials; new buildings glint with glass panes, the antithesis of the secluded Arab architecture persevered for a thousand years. Recklessly things are torn down and put up all over the place. Streets have new Arabic names, old French names, sometimes both, frequently neither. Crowds form at the

drop of a hat: a bicycle race spreads up and down the main street and everyone lines up on the sidewalk to watch, at midnight.

In the part of town where construction has not sprouted in the vacant
lots prepared for it, there is a slapdash carnival with bright lights, rides, games
and sideshows. Its perimeter is the vague outline reached by its lights, and
swarms of children hang about it like summer moths. There is no need to go
there with a child of your own; I discovered that you can hire one as soon as
you step out of the surrounding darkness.

I am surprised to enter these pages now holding a child's hand. When I
crossed that carnival threshold a recent summer's night in Tangier, I felt a
tug on my arm as I gazed with wonder at a sign on top of a battered bus
converted to hold a sideshow. THE SNAKE LADY, it read, ALIVE. The sign
painter had created a voluptuous creature more Danish than Arabic who lay
entwined in the torrid and not altogether reptilian embrace of a boa con-
strictor the size of a large man. I thought that the tug, at first, was some
flinch of my own. It was repeated twice. I looked down, locating among the
crowd pressing forward a little girl wearing a blue sailor suit, her head
framed by a pair of dark pigtails. On her shoulder she carried an oversized
pocketbook of black plastic which may have been her mother's, mirroring
the bright bulbs around us.

"Yes?" I asked, avuncular. "What would you like?" I saw that Spanish
had no effect. I reached into my small fund of Arabic.

There was a sudden smile revealing a double blank in her upper front
teeth. Then the face dropped, all downcast eyes, and I turned back to the
sign.

"Do you want to see the Snake Lady?" I asked over my shoulder.

She nodded energetically behind her pocketbook.

"Isn't your, ah, family here?"

She shook her head. Again I had a chance to see the missing space in her
grin. "My sister," she said, and from out of the crush, in a larger dimension,
her duplicate appeared. She, too, had braids. But her smile was more hesi-
tant, more cautious.

"Are there any more of you?"

They shook their heads no, and three of us got in line, joined all at once
by a small boy who must have been watching the negotiations. He, too, was
desperate to see the Snake Lady. He, too, beamed a smile upwards. We just
made it through the doll's door of the reconverted bus as other kids came running.

A monkey balanced a banana on his knees but no one watched, for all
heads were bent forward, magnetized by the Snake Lady in the aisle beyond. Spying her, the boy nudged me, his cheeks bright pink with embar-
rassment. The girls giggled. There she was, squeezed into a coffin-like space
covered by a pane of glass smudged with fingerprints. She was wearing what

were once called hot pants and her blouse was scooped low. The snake was asleep, stretched from the edge of the box past her thighs to her neck, and she held up its head to the crowd as though displaying some kitchen utensil. She was beyond boredom, beyond sadness or despair. Pressed against the glass were veiled ladies who are permitted to place only their eyes on view. Half dressed, she looked languidly at them. Bundled, they looked fearfully at her. She alone knew what strange construction of fate had gotten her into this terrible, airless predicament: to lie on display with a snake asleep on her, for coins.

"Take a picture!" pleaded one of my group, swaying impatiently behind her large pocketbook. I obliged by picking up the camera almost to eye level. The drowsy girl with the snake lifted one finger, wagged it back and forth in a gesture as grand as any ex-President's wife that said: *no pictures, please.* And as we turned to leave the rank bus, I waved to her. Immediately, she flashed a heartbreaking smile at me, let the snake's head drop and closed her eyes, blocking out the whole catastrophe. I realized then that she was only about sixteen, made up and bleached to look thirty-five. The paying customers knocked against the glass, pressing palms along its surface: men in coarse burnooses in from the countryside, their women peering eternally with those exposed eyes, jabbering to each other in bird voices, and kids punching the sides of the bus and stamping their feet with impatience to be grownup, to inhabit the heady Western world which included in it ladies all exposed like this. Slowly, very slowly, she sat upright, resumed her position and looked into the middle distance. She picked up the snake again, pressing its cold head to her cheek, and the crowd, satisfied, filed by.

"Where are your parents?" I asked again as we emerged from the bus and headed towards the rides.

The boy interrupted, requiring some money to see the death-defying motorcycle act. Then he rushed off with the money and lost himself in the crowd.

"Home," said the elder.

"Home," said the younger. "I'd like some ice cream."

"Well, why aren't you home with them?" I asked, suddenly angry. The girls were wandering around bumping into strangers; the boy had gone off to see spinning motorcycles at one in the morning.

"Why aren't *you* home?" asked the younger sister, swaying from side to side, hugging her plastic pocketbook.

I had no proper answer. Why wasn't everyone else home—the girl with the snake, or the snake itself? I was in a land of truants. And in my bad temper I left the two sisters to wander around until dawn if they chose, and went in search of a drink, climbing the famous sloping streets towards the center of the new town. There I located the bar-restaurant that is the local international meeting ground. Foreginers who have many years of drinking

behind them and not many ahead stared into their own reflections in the long bar mirror. Local boys speaking many languages decorated the place too engagingly, their voices like silk, their eyes cutting and recutting across the room like busy teletype machines. Presiding over it all was a frizzy-haired lady, a foreigner, whose lower lip pouted like an open purse. It was depressing. Everyone was up too late, trying to make things last too long. In Spain, whose habits Tangier has adopted, the late-night promenades seem in character.

Here in Africa the nocturnal activity has an air of delinquency. Night and morning overlap publicly. The long moment of complete silence and immobility remains unobserved. Rif mountain women begin to arrive at the markets while it is still dark, their goods, like sleeping children, bundled over their backs. Yawns from a night's sleep in the kasbah cross with yawns from not having yet been to bed in the new town. Stalls creak open, cocks crow and dogs yap while cars are still tearing around corners searching out mischief. It is the irregular envelope of Africa being torn open at its edge before it has been properly sealed for the night.

I lay in my hotel room wondering about the little girl's question, "Why aren't *you* home?" Then I went to the window. A group of drunken foreigners had rounded the corner singing.

"The fundamental things apply . . ."

"A sigh is just a sigh . . ."

"No, a sigh is *still* a sigh."

"I'll sing it as I please."

They continued down the street, the shreds of *As Time Goes By* almost obscuring the distant dawn chant of the muezzin summoning Moslems to prayer, the *Allah akbar*, God is great, rising like smoke from the old town. And I thought, looking out at the black rooftops, searching for some sign of light in the sky, that time certainly had gone by.

Islam is defined as submission to God's will, implying no need to chart time into mortal margins. In the Tangier railroad station, the clock tells the hour in an appropriate manner. When it moves, the minute hand jolts too far ahead, too far to the right. Then it slides backwards into place. You might look up to see a minute moving in reverse or you might catch it as it moves too quickly forward. You have the uneasy sensation that time is a personal, random thing, not a mathematical division carefully worked out to organize our planet. This disorientation will do as a metaphor for Morocco, for North Africa and for the rest of the Moslem world.

One door of a pair leading to the station platform is slowly opened to the waiting room. A station attendant wearing several elements of a mainly khaki uniform has peered around the corner. Now he stands looking belligerent, his ticket puncher poised like a weapon. Instantly he is mobbed by the horde of passengers who want to board the train. The crush at the station is stupefying. Veiled women step on each other's toes, rebuking each other like crows. Most of them are wearing the latest in heavy clogs beneath the crafty shapelessness of their garments. Moroccan youths in blue jeans, valises perched on their heads, push hard against each other to scrimmage for that one door. People carrying babies hold them up as armor; small children nip at heels and thighs; the foreign visitors remain at the edge of the swollen mass, their mouths gaping wide like beached fish. They are hooked with astonishment onto their belongings and their apprehension. A hippie contingent is splayed in disarray against the walls.

"John, *for God's sake* get up!"

Bent, her bottom wagging, a pretty English girl wearing a fringed miniskirt shakes a crouched object, a male, on a pile of luggage.

There is no answer. There will be no answer. She stands straight, putting her hands on her hips, waiting. She has gone to good schools. She has been given a reasonable allowance. And she is not prepared to disintegrate in North Africa with a drug addict.

"We shall miss the bloody train!" she says severely.

There is a long pause. Then she bends to shriek in his ear: "FREAK!"

He tries to rise, remembering obedience from some earlier time, sits again, receives a shake from his girl friend, stands, sprawls against a collection of robed figures who buffer him like a truckload of laundry. The spaced-out 1970's ramming into descendants of the Merinid dynasty (fourteenth century), when private deeds were never aired, misconduct was never public and artists were paid in gold dust. When he is back again on his valise, the frieze of Arabs look at him, at her; quickly at each other, at the ceiling and beyond, where Allah dwells, He who is all-merciful, all-compassionate.

The crowd thickens. John and his girl friend are obscured by the latecomers rushing in. The man at the door in his incomplete uniform takes his time examining each and every ticket. He studies, he fusses, he checks dates and destinations. He is finally shoved aside by a band of kids making a desperate goal. Just as quickly they are heaved back into the waiting room by a larger guard lurking behind the other door. Slowly, slowly as the minutes pass, everyone is allowed to ooze through onto the platform. There are the bruised, now complaining, now with an audience; there are cries of recognition from long-lost friends, and there are eyes slitted down at newfound enemies. But there is no train. The train, though, was not what everyone was fighting for: it was the battle to see who would precede whom through the door that interested them. Dusk begins to settle on the city as passengers pace the platform waiting stoically for their train, which is an hour late. Only the foreigners complain.

The clock now bounces forward and slides back to an empty room. The water sellers—with their gleaming brass bowls, their leather casks and tasseled outfits—have gone; so has the almond vendor, the pair of gumsellers, the pickpockets, the loiterers, and those who have come to participate in the goings-away. John and his girl friend have been taken by the police into a back room, where only her *for God's sake* can be heard, muffled, her plea to her Allah. A waiting room—any waiting room—is carved out of suspended time. Everyone assembled there has begun to move out of their pasts. Their goodbyes are finished. They wait. They are accumulating their hellos for the

other end. And some of them doze, mired into the parenthesis.

In the Arab world the art of waiting is learned like a skill; one has the opportunity to practice it several times a day. It was almost night when the train finally arrived. The crowd once again was roused into chaos, scrambling on board, rushing to get seats, reminding each other that manners have nothing to do with ticket-class distinctions when push, as they say, comes to shove.

"It is occupied," said a plump woman with a Marseillaise accent just as I was about to ease myself into a vacant space beside her. "I wouldn't dream of giving up this seat," she continued, "for . . . for all the gold in the world!" She then moved over to take possession of both seats, sitting between them, slightly expanding her person in the process.

Was it her banality or her brass that brought me close to throwing myself into her lap? During the split second of this decision I was pushed off balance by the general rush of passengers through the aisles. Luggage dug into my calves, elbows prodded my ribs, a shouted quartet of languages assaulted my ears. Tangier's station began to slide away as the train slowly gained momentum. There was no giving this departure its proper due. I saw that I was destined to spend the five-hour journey to Casablanca wedged into the aisle. But then, with no logic, in true Mediterranean fashion, a seat was swiftly vacated in front of me and I hurled myself into it with no thought of good manners or bad but only of survival. Holding fast to the armrests, my new territory, I tried to block out the commotion. Outside the window the modern suburbs stalked across rubbly fields. There was no further hope of seeing the town. Wide beaches on my left, then the Straits of Gibraltar beyond, then the coast of Europe. The last shred of Tangier vanished around a corner.

Imagine Hercules on these plains. Here at Lixus the legend is that he battled Antaeus the giant, son of Poseidon, and won. Crushing his opponent, Hercules then quickly lifted him off the ground—for Antaeus' mother was Mother Earth and she might have revived him—to hold him aloft while he died, the countryside echoing with his mighty groans. The land seems quite gentle now. The Maghreb, or more properly the Maghreb el Aksa, the Land of the Farthest West, is an ancient land. For more than three thousand years it is supposed to have been inhabited. Skeletons of the Neanderthal period were unearthed in its caves. Great age hides out there, and bloody battles, and betrayals and cruelty few lands have seen. The softness of the early summer evening rocking past the train window is suspect. For fifty years, from 1672, Moulay Ismail reigned as Sultan of the 'Alawids. He killed his subjects to amuse himself. Galloping past his ranks, he would behead or disembowel any of them he fancied dead. If they became too tired or too weak while constructing palace walls, slaves and prisoners were built into the surfaces where they fell. It is said that Moulay Ismail instituted reforms throughout his domain, that robbery was no longer to be feared, that crops were abundant. But no one looked forward to an old age.

"I'm *eighty. J'ai quatre-vingt ans!*" shouted a Viennese in the aisle behind me. "He MUST give me his seat! Eighty! Do I make myself clear?"

I looked back cautiously over my shoulder. I did not wish to get involved. In New York we are supposed to bypass bodies on the street. I saw a white-haired man with flushed cheeks, someone who might have made many enemies in his lifetime. His rage was not at all mollified by the complete passivity of the Negro woman to whom he was appealing. She sat wearing a crisp kaftan. Next to her, fidgeting, on his own seat, was her young son.

"I have paid for two tickets," she said solemnly, "and he will stay in his seat."

"How can you dare?" the Viennese shouted, addressing himself now to the other passengers. All conversation stopped. Africa rolled by unnoticed.

"Tell the child to give up his seat," said a seated, rather grand Italian lady with a Milanese accent. "Immediately . . ." she added, rummaging through a handbag for a gold cigarette lighter.

The black woman stared out of the window and drew a metaphoric veil of passivity over herself that did not quite cover the restless child next to her.

Hasty allegiances were formed in their vicinity. The Milanese woman inhaled her cigarette, said "*Disgraziata,*" to the air and fanned away the smoke. The elderly gentleman accumulated an unhealthy shade of purple on his face and there was an intake of breath from the passengers. The mechanical sounds of the train rattled loudly.

At that moment a conductor came through and listened with great patience while the situation was explained, with various degrees of passion and emphasis, by the foreigners near the eye of the storm. The man's great age was established as remarkable. The necessity for him to have a seat was repeated; the Arab child's needlessly occupying a space that might have served a foreign adult was examined, as was the mother's irritating detachment: all of it held everyone's interest for quite a while. The conductor stood in the aisle listening gravely. A nomad chieftain could not have seemed more impartial. Would he side with the Arab woman in a show of *asabiyya* (loyalty)? Would he, in a surge of *diyafa* (hospitality), suggest that the foreigner be given a seat? Would he find yet another solution which would save the face (*wajh*) and maintain the honor (*sharaf*) of both parties involved? All these heralded bedouin virtues were suspended in the air as the train raced through the flat country.

In American English he said, "It's not my problem." Then he continued down the aisle. "It's your problem," he said as he left them behind.

The Viennese went ashen. There was an agitated murmur of worry around him. Prodded by a relative, a young French girl stood up with petu-

lance and offered the man her seat. He thanked her curtly—why had she waited so long?—and crumpled himself down. Everyone slowly cooled. The General Assembly at the United Nations would have recessed for lunch.

"Whose side were you on? You, you, *usted?*"

I had been too absorbed to realize that the small low-browed woman across the aisle was addressing me.

"The woman with the child," I said. "An eighty-year-old man should stay out of Africa in the summer."

"Your Spanish sounds Mexican," she said. "You go *up* at the end of a sentence." Her tiny index finger drew a large comma up in the air.

There was no time to work out an answer. She had already embarked on the story of her life. In rapid succession she reported that she was Jewish, born in Madrid, moved to Casablanca, raised many children, ran a pension, lost a husband, sold the pension—And here she stopped, fumbled in her large straw bag, located her purse and withdrew from it the family photographs, handed across the aisle to me like a deck of worn cards from a magician's pocket. Quickly these were followed by the smallest of address books

—she was by now standing in the aisle—in which each child's address was located, then indicated by that same tiny index finger.

They all smiled up through the adroit retouching. Yes, they were each beautiful. Yes, I did know where some of the addresses were, and they were good addresses, too. She sat back in her seat, satisfied, her toes tapping the floor, rumbling across the African plains. She seemed so small and frail to have created this international network of related genes: London, Argentina, New York . . .

The train whistle hooted as we rounded a curve and we sped past a small village station, consuming it in a blur to leave behind the memory of a desolate platform.

"There is a draft!" announced the woman with the Milanese accent.

"Close the door!" commanded the Viennese from his seat.

But by now everyone had lost interest in him. So, huffing and puffing mightily, he himself came down the aisle to the door at the end of the car, just in front of my seat. He pulled on the door. It would not close. There was an Arab's foot in the doorway. The rest of the person was wedged into the corridor beyond, opposite the toilet.

"You cannot close it," said the Spanish lady reasonably.

"I will close it," said the Viennese. "There is a draft."

"There is someone standing there," she said, "*someone who did not get a seat the way you did.*"

The Viennese said something unintelligible pulling the door against the foot. And at this point, unexpectedly, I stood, my feet barely touching the floor as I whirled the old gentleman around and sent him angrily back to his seat. Then I said, "Now, stay in it."

With a remarkable slowness, the Arab's foot changed position. Then there was a worn pants leg, a torso clad in a jacket from another suit, and finally a face appeared around the corner. It was an old-young face, and on top of it was a fez. The apparition quickly withdrew after sizing me up, then reappeared, and, after another moment, with no ceremony at all, slid with a suitcase into a squatting position in front of me. The door swung closed behind him.

"Rachid," he said. It sounded like a sneeze.

I introduced myself.

At this point I must interrupt the narrative to mention to the reader that there is little value to the word "Arab." Originally—but this is twenty-seven centuries ago—the word referred to desert people, nomads who roamed Africa and Asia. Arab is still the collective word for tents. Long after, in the mid-seventh century, when Mohammed's teachings took hold throughout the Arabian Peninsula and spread throughout the Mediterranean, the term Arab became synonymous with the followers of Islam—the Koran is always recited in Arabic—and the diverse tribes, races and nationalities were joined together by the language.

Think of Arabs, then, as people primarily sharing a language, even though the many forms of it and the dialects are frequently unrecognizable from one Arab country to the next. Then think of the Arabs as a people who share a religion, although this, too, is not altogether true. There are many Christian Arabs; there are Egyptian Copts; Jews live in Arab lands and hold their nation's passports but they are known there as Jews. You might also think of the Arabs as a kind of brotherhood of tradition and politics, an amorphous, non-geographical nation. Ideally, this would make everything easier—both for our comprehension and for the Arabs themselves, who are most of the time battling with the country bordering their own.

Finally, it must be remembered that there really is no longer an Arab race. Hittites, Sumerians, Philistines, Phoenicians, Persians and Vandals colonized the Arab world, as did Greeks and Romans, Central Africans, Turks, Armenians, Kurds, the French, the Spanish, the Portuguese, the English . . . In addition, there were, and still are, the pale Berbers forever roaming North Africa, always somewhat apart, their origins permanently mysterious. There is, then, no Arab race, unless the descendants of the Arabian Peninsula are to be considered a race still. The best that can be said for the word is that *Arab* is a state of mind, with the loosest of racial connections, that thinks in a common language.

Rachid inquired about the health of my family and I inquired about his. Both of us, it seemed, had healthy families. The Spanish woman was included. Her photographs were not produced again, though her hand strayed into her bag. She brought out some bunches of grapes. I looked out of my window. The apoplectic rage behind me had subsided now that the door had closed. The Milanese woman had fallen asleep after reconfirming her stand on matters relating to the comfort of the principal travelers. The lights were dimmed in our car. Our train gained momentum, passing a series of stilled, third-class wooden compartments on a siding. Ghostly silhouettes leaned from its windows. Soon they were left behind, a phantom railway imprisoned in the Moroccan night.

"I have a telephone in my furniture factory," said Rachid as I was about to doze.

"Ah."

It was a lame reaction. He looked crestfallen.

"I can call you in America," he said.

"I have a son in America," said the woman. "In Flushing." She pronounced it Flooshin.

"My brother has been to America," said Rachid with importance.

"Perhaps he has met my son," said the Spanish woman, offering him some grapes.

Rachid took them and passed the rest to me. He then threw his pits and branches into the aisle. The Spanish woman watched him do this. When he was through she got up with a grunt, picked the residue off the floor and deposited it into a wastebasket. There was no word of reproof. She had lived long in these parts. She returned to her seat and went immediately to sleep, snoring with enthusiasm. Refusing my seat, Rachid, kneeling still, stared into space. The compartment became a moving ward. Occasional villages passed, illuminated by slender streetamps; then blackness. Other trains streaked by screaming; our car rocked in their wake, then it was silent. In vain did I try to sleep.

"RABAT," someone announced, and there was a stirring and shuffling in the aisle. "The lovely twin cities of Salé the white and Rabat the red frown at each other over the foaming bar of the Bou Regreg," wrote Edith Wharton in her 1925 *In Morocco*, "each walled, terraced, minareted, and presenting a singularly complete picture of the two types of Moroccan town, the snowy and the tawny."

And Robinson Crusoe was a slave here. I got up and stretched.

"You will visit my factory in Casa," said Rachid. It was not a question.

I said that I would.

"My brother has been to America. He will want to meet you."

The train started up again. I ached. I was red-eyed. In theory I love trains, but actually I rarely enjoy riding on them. I longed for a hotel bed and some privacy.

"You will meet my brother who has been to America," he stated.

I would have promised anything to be left alone in silence.

"Tomorrow," he said, and he fell asleep on his haunches.

Chapter Two

CASABLANCA AND RABAT

I am always in a hurry in Casablanca, hurrying, usually, to get out of town. *Casablanca*: the name implies a world of cinematic romance and intrigue no other city can hope to match. But the actual movie of that name was not made there and has never been shown in Morocco. The Chamber of Commerce did not recognize a good thing when it came its way.

The Spanish gave the city—then a village—its name, retreating before Moulay Ismail in the eighteenth century, leaving behind a small port on the Atlantic battered by high seas, so small that atlases of a century ago do not list it on Africa's shore. In 1906, when twenty-five thousand people lived there, French engineers were given permission by the Sultan to construct a harbor in Casablanca. The Moroccans rioted. No one fully understood how the crisis came about, but nine workmen were killed, there were reports that a Moslem woman was raped; looting followed, and burning. And French troops arrived to control the disorder. They would stay, with varying degrees of authority, for fifty years.

Casablanca thrived under the French. A harbor was eventually constructed to tame the Atlantic with extra-long jetties. It would become the greatest port in the Maghreb, larger than Oran or Tunis. Now the population is almost two million. Although the French have withdrawn from Morocco, their investments in Casablanca's industries remain.

It is called simply Casa by those who know it, depriving the name of all the atmosphere the city possibly never had. Travel writers have usually avoided it; guidebooks try to give it an appropriate amount of space: Fodor tells you that its "sights" can be seen in a morning. Tourists go there to change trains and planes, transsexuals go there to change genders, others pass through to straighten out tickets, collect mail or take a hot bath. It is almost impossible to circumvent it once you have entered Morocco, like trying to avoid the Winged Victory once inside the Louvre.

The morning following my arrival there, Rachid was standing just outside my hotel's double doors watching with interest as a porter polished the brass fittings. He wore the same mismatching suit and the same crestfallen expression. There was no telling how long he had been there. His patience had been established as remarkable the night before on the train.

"I've come," he said portentously, "to present you to my younger brother."

I looked at the area next to him. It was empty.

"No time now," I said with determination. I had arranged that morning to pick up a car and get out of town, deluding myself—Western notions die hard—that it would be ready for me.

"He's just a few steps away," he said. "He's been to America. He wants to wish you well."

"I . . ."

"You promised, *without question*," he interrupted. "Yesterday on the train."

My mouth was still open to form its excuses. "Ah, yes," it said instead.

"At our factory, we have a telephone."

"I remember," I said enthusiastically. Then I added, "In France it takes five years to get a telephone."

"I can call Paris," he said.

We crossed the square in front of the hotel by proceeding down a flight of steps into a newly built subterranean sidewalk with a varicolored dome set in its center. Traffic swirled overhead. I do not like to cross streets underground and said so, though the blameless tunnel had nothing to do with my gathering predicament.

"This is new," he replied, "and modern."

"But . . ." I began, sidestepping the shower from an underground fountain beneath the dome.

"As you said about telephones," he continued, "this city is more advanced than Paris. Half the electrical power of Morocco"—he stepped across a figure lying on the tiles—"is consumed by Casablanca."

A lame child next to a wall, begging, made an abrupt move and dropped his coins into a sewer. He looked down the drain without complaint and dragged himself on.

"Casablanca possibly has better electricity," said Rachid, "than Paris."

The morning was gradually taking on the surreal aspect I always encounter in the Arab world and have never managed to take for granted. We had emerged from the tunnel in front of the town's newest hotel. Visitors were just rousing themselves from their air-conditioned, soundproofed sleep while, outside, decades tumbled like dominoes as old walls fell under housewrecking equipment.

"New," said Rachid, "all new."

We walked quickly past the hotel's new boutiques where kaftans cost, I

noticed, a local month's wages and then some. Soon we were on the streets that were barely paved, outlined by torn and shredded buildings. A line of five blind men walked uncertainly around a corner, with detached dignity while everyone else hurried along. Their voices as they chanted *"Allah"* in unison were harsh and guttural. Each of them thrust out a tin plate and withdrew it, thrusting it out again in a tragic parody of a chorus line.

When I found myself uselessly saying that I did not have any time for this excursion, Rachid quickened his pace, as though his determination alone would bridge the distance between us and his fabled brother. Now we would crowd against walls to let a donkey pass, now we would hop across large puddles and cave-ins on what was the street.

"Just a few steps away," he said, dashing ahead of me.

We passed schoolboys in airless rooms shouting the verses of the Koran, sounding, by their enthusiasm, like spectators at a soccer match; we passed piles of bright plastic bottles teetering on top of a mule cart; automobile fenders were being hammered into shape in a vacant lot; and a striped cat streaked across in front of us pursuing a rodent the size of a chihuahua. And still no brother, no furniture factory.

"It's not possible," I said finally, standing still to catch my breath. "We've crossed half the town."

"There!" cried Rachid in triumph, and he ran across the street to disappear into a garage.

His brother, bowing low over a Singer sewing machine, had not exactly *been* to America. His brother, extending a hand, rising with smiles on his intense young face, *liked* Americans. His brother, motioning me into the furniture storeroom in back of the garage, piled high with matching leatherette chairs and settees, had never actually *met* an American. But he knew them from the movies.

"I've been had," I said aloud to myself.

"I've been had," said he, repeating it perfectly to Rachid. Then he asked me what it meant. In addition to Americans, it seemed, he liked the American language as well.

"Something you say to yourself," I answered, after considering it, "when you're at the will of a Higher Power."

They seemed pleased with that. Around the storage room, chairs were stacked to the ceiling, settees were upended and clustered together, all the same, all tufted black leatherette. The Islamic tradition is that once a pattern is established, it is repeated over and over again until forcibly stopped. I found myself suppressing a fit of unkind laughter at my circumstances and covered it by taking a few deep breaths.

"Rushing, rushing," said Rachid.

"You must relax," said the brother. "You Americans are always rushing. In your Westerns, you are always rushing on your horses, and in your crime movies you are always rushing in your automobiles. Robert Redford, too, was always rushing in *The Sting*. And James Bond can never keep still. You could be a cowboy or a James Bond type, eh, Rachid?"

"You must have an Orange Crush," said Rachid, not committing himself.

The brother returned to his sewing machine and proceeded to squeeze oil into its motor. Rachid was dispatched to find a small boy who would then be sent to fetch the drink. I sat on a vacant chair, my eyes scanning the dark cavern.

"You have a lot of furniture," I observed unnecessarily.

"Business is bad. But we are going to add a new piece to our collection."

I asked what that would be.

"A sofa. Of black leatherette. We have a good connection here in Casablanca who can get it for us. A cousin. A black sofa, to match the rest."

He walked over to perch on the arm of a settee.

"Now," he said, "tell me about America."

I groaned into the black leatherette. I thought of Sir Richard Burton in his flowing garb, his caravans, his pilgrim ships, his daggers and his battles: "To do our enemy justice, they showed no sign of flinching; they swarmed towards the poop like angry hornets, and encouraged each other with cries of *Allaho akbar!* But we had a vantage-ground about four feet above them, and their palm-sticks and short daggers could do nothing against our quarter-staves."* And here was I, sitting in the near dark of a storeroom launching into an earnest discussion of movies and blue jeans.

Then there was the ceremonial serving of the Orange Crush. When the boy finally arrived with the bottle in its largest dimension, he placed it on top of a chair's arm and walked out, back into the streets, leaving it there unopened. Would it open itself? Having satisfied himself about the availability of women, clothes, about building heights and the proliferation of Organized Crime in America, the brother returned to his sewing machine and started up the motor, testing a thread through a scrap of that same black material. Rachid smiled and tapped his fingers. The machine hummed. And I waited, wondering, at that moment, whether someone had jammed the film of the Casablanca sequence, abandoning me to spend the rest of my days in Africa sitting on a section of a living-room suite in a dank storeroom in back of a garage on a side street near the center of town waiting to be offered a glass of that bright, bilious liquid. I looked at my watch rudely, and stood to leave.

"What, leaving?" asked Rachid. He had been staring into space.

The brother said, "But you have just arrived."

I said, "It's time, it's time." I looked out into the street with something resembling anguish.

With a sigh, Rachid got up and began to search for the bottle opener. Then we all three toasted each other, our respective families and Rachid's wife and children—none of whom had previously been mentioned. There was a long silence while we assiduously savored the drink, broken at last by the younger brother, who decided, now that he had met his first American, that he might begin a correspondence with another one—a girl perhaps; possibly a blonde. He could, he told me, even telephone her. I was shown the telephone. A little lock was on its dial. I made appropriate sounds, a kind of hum.

When I went out of the door, both brothers looked crestfallen. I realized, then, that the look was a formality. Rachid accompanied me on the complicated route back to the hotel. We passed everything in reverse, as though time had stopped: the fenders were still being hammered, the boys bellowed the Koran, the blind led the blind. At the doors of the hotel, the porter was staring at the shining knob he had just completed polishing. I tried

* Sir Richard Burton, *Pilgrimage to Al-Madinah and Meccah*, Vol. I (New York: Dover).

to think of something to say to have made Rachid's hospitality seem worthwhile.

"I'll call," I said, holding, in my American way, an imagined receiver up to my ear. "I'll call you on your telephone."

He smiled wanly, rightfully unconvinced.

"*Un grand bonjour à votre famille,*" he said.

"And to yours."

"And to your parents."

"And to your wife and child."

He hesitated. "I've been had," he said, waving one more time before retreating down the street.

But I was not to leave Casablanca, not quite yet. There are places and people put in our paths whose only purpose in our lives is to detain us. I was reminded of this again at the counter of the automobile rental office.

"You had said my car would be ready."

"Tomorrow."

"Tomorrow is not today, as you had said."

"Tomorrow, today, it is the same. It doesn't make any difference."

"It does to me. I planned on being in Rabat this evening."

"Casablanca has many night spots. They come from Algeria, where there is no night life. They come from all over. International."

"About the car."

"Tomorrow. It is our best car and I have reserved it for you. The one I could give you today is inferior."

"I'll take today's car."

"But I wouldn't think of it! Such an esteemed person as yourself should not drive such a car. Besides, you would look—if you will forgive me—foolish in it. You are tall. Very tall. Like a cowboy. It is a tiny car."

"Let me see it."

"It isn't here. Come back tomorrow. Tomorrow's car is your car."

In the evening I was in the fashionable suburbs of Casablanca wondering why I had accepted an invitation to a small party when I knew—and only vaguely—a cousin of the man who was the host. Among Arabs, the number of ersatz cousins makes large families seem even larger still. A light rain had begun to fall and the heavy scent of datura and jasmine hugged the night air. A quantity of fancy cars glistened beneath the streetlamps. All was quiet except for the rain and the party sounds that came inevitably from the terrace to which I was heading.

The television set was on full blast; so was the phonograph. The host smiled and extended a big butcher's hand, asking immediate forgiveness for not having the time to introduce me around. He was grilling meats—Texas style, he said—on the terrace. A dozen or so people lounged around shouting loudly above the two appliances. I glanced at the television screen to see a turbaned youth suffering against a pitted wall.

"It's *imPOSSible*," crooned an American singer from the phonograph. The image on the screen changed. Now a woman wearing a diaphanous veil lamented into a rosebush.

"It's *imPOSSible* . . ."

"They never kiss," said a girl with long hair, which she twined around her fingers.

"Never?"

The host crossed between us wearing a Bar B Que apron, winked, and went onto the terrace to turn the kabobs.

"Not in these Egyptian films about classic love," she said.

"They're so totally *boring*," said another girl over her shoulder as she bent to change the record.

"That's better," she said. "*Woh-man, take me in yoah ahms and rock me, babeh*," now blared across the room. The television set abruptly surrendered to the competition and now presented a series of frenzied lines, then a brief, sharp picture of a tree, its branches uplifted, beseeching; then it went blank.

It was not long before I, too, began to go blank. The drinking and noise and smoke successfully managed to eradicate any sense of place. Moroccans are fobidden by the Koran to drink alcohol the way Americans are forbidden by law to smoke dope, and these laws are as carefully observed in one country as they are in the other.

Following the party—my mind dims when I try to remember it—we got into fast cars and went off to a private club on the outer reaches of the windswept corniche that fronts the Atlantic. The rain, the methodic wind-shield wipers, the blurred headlights, the combination of phonograph, television, whiskey, kif, and babbling turned me into a mute. I was no addition to anyone's party. I left the private club—complete with Prohibition peephole—got into a taxi and found myself in the center of Casablanca in front of a nightclub the taxi driver kept repeating was authentic.

"A nightclub?" I asked.

"You kept saying *authentic*," he said, "authentic Moroccans, authentic music. I thought I'd bring you here."

I thanked him, held my head in an attempt to clear it and stood listening to the music echoing unhealthily up the stairs from the nightclub. Inside, the place was empty except for one table of Algerians celebrating a birthday. The musicians each wore a glazed look: they might as well have been typing letters. An energetic belly dancer parted the curtains, noted with dismay the paucity of the crowd, but nonetheless—brave girl—entered the stage with a searing ululation, clacking her tongue furiously behind the back of her raised hand. The Algerians watched with apathy.

"What are you looking for?" asked the cashier, moving towards me at the bar. I said that I was too far gone to look for much of anything, that the Moroccans could outdrink and outsmoke me anytime.

She turned away slowly, gigantic in a metallic sweater, grazing me. Our sweaters briefly warmed.

"Is that an oud?" I asked, pointing to one of the instruments.

"It's slow tonight," she said, not having heard.

I agreed, she yawned, the musicians kept playing, the girl kept dancing.

"Maybe Arab music is going out of style," said the cashier, about to swivel my way again. "This place used to be filled with busloads. Hotels sent them over."

She had said the magic word: hotel. Now I remembered where I was going. I asked her for directions. The dancer was about to liquefy, the musicians had turned to stone. The cashier's sigh filled the air and the eyebrow she raised reached up and joined her jet-black hairline: Such were my perceptions.

My mistake was that I decided to return to the hotel on foot. I have trouble, as you will see, even in the best of times, concentrating on directions. I often study the stranger giving them to me and forget whatever it is he is saying. I did remember that the cashier had said there was a bank on the corner. A *bank on the corner*, I said to myself, only to realize that I was on a corner with the wrong bank. The Casablanca streets—famous for romance and intrigue—were empty. The day had been too long. I could not accommodate the sequences, join them in a logical ribbon of time. The lone image of the black-and-white tree presented by the television screen before going blank seemed the one shred of reality.

"You want a good time?"

I turned to see two girls, veiled, standing next to each other in a doorway. They were pretty—that is, their eyes were pretty—and they were slim and very young. The robes they wore almost touched the wet sidewalk.

I think at first that I said no, I had no need of a good time, and I began to set off in some mistaken direction. It must have been obvious because I hesitated.

"Are you lost?" one of them asked, a pink blur.

"Yes," I said angrily. "Yes," I repeated more pleasantly.

She asked me where I lived. I told her.

"Come along, it's not far," she said. Then she laughed, a high-pitched little girl's laugh, and left her friend to take my arm. We did not go to my hotel, we went to hers, a small place down a side street whose sign was only in Arabic. Even the Coca-Cola poster behind the rickety front desk was only in Arabic.

"Authentic," I said to the disagreeable man slouched behind the desk in his soiled kaftan. He grunted and handed me some keys.

I remember my surprise when I discovered that underneath her robes was a pair of quaint bloomers with a floral pattern that, in my muddled state, brought me back along a shadowy path to some childhood wallpaper in a summer house. But I soon forgot about place and time and sequence moving into that perishable, Islamic state of timelessness.

"Tomorrow," she said later, "we can bring my friend from the corner. She's nice, too."

"Tomorrow," I said, "I will be gone."

There was a pause. The flowered bloomers rustled.

"Money for the man downstairs," she said brusquely. "If not, he makes troubles."

I sighed involuntarily, finally sobered.

"And for the person who makes up the room. And for my friend who didn't come along, who would have come tomorrow, who was left on the streetcorner alone and had to go home."

"Anyone else?" I asked, weary.

"Let me think," she said, and she proceeded to think, sitting back down on the bed.

"I was misinformed," I said in English to the flaking walls.

"You American?" she asked, surprised. "I thought you were French." She stood up to study me.

I thought of evading the question, remembering Rachid's brother in that faraway morning.

"American," I said stoutly. It sounded oddly reassuring.

"Then forget the money for all the others. They owe me favors anyway. **An** American piece of clothes will do. My size."

"I don't happen to have . . ."

"Blue jeans, I can cut smaller. Shoes, of course, are no good. Let me think . . ." She prepared to seat herself again on the bed.

"In fact, I have something," I said, pulling her towards me.

"No joking now. This is the clothes part."

"But I really have," I said.

When we hurried out of the hotel door, the man at the front desk came shambling after us demanding money.

"I'll tell him you were poor. A poor American." Then she laughed in her girlish treble.

"Just keep laughing," I said.

She stood outside those same double doors of my hotel, shy of coming in, standing, oddly, in just the place Rachid had chosen. I remember going up to my room, rummaging through my suitcase, returning downstairs past the man drowsing at the front desk to hand her a small package. In it was a pale blue T-shirt, secreted into my luggage by an enterprising friend as I left New

York. It said on the shirt: Hold me
                            squeeze me
                            take me home.
I translated as she held it up to herself, posing before her reflection in the hotel doors. She laughed, turning this way and that.

"An advertisement," she said finally. "Very good for just under the veil."

And she danced on the steps to no music. The streets had dried from the rain, there was not a car, not a sound, not another figure moving, it seemed, in all of Casablanca. The first light of dawn was in the sky as I watched her vanish around the corner, the package hidden under her robes, a delicate figure out of the *Thousand and One Nights* who would perish in the bright light of day.

In Rabat, I dealt with officials.

Round and round I drove, trying to locate a certain minister. The same manicured lawns kept reappearing on either side of the road, the same embassies and grand houses. And the same uniformed guards. They began to suspect something about my driving by so frequently. No one sane could have been that lost.

"Where are the offices of X?" I continued to ask.

"That way. No, that way . . ."

I drove on. Suddenly a jumble of office buildings would loom up: new, official, stark. Just as suddenly the road would end, I would put the car into reverse and begin all over again. Flags flew from tall posts. Rabat is Morocco's capital. The King is here. The University is here. It is where the employed Americans live. Its new streets are set out like fishhooks.

"*Non, il n'est· pas là,*" said a gentleman in uniform at an information desk.

"Do you mean that he is not *in?* Or do you mean that his offices are not *here?*" I was beginning to speak with a dangerous rasp in my voice.

"*Là, là!*" he answered angrily, only to confuse me further. Although *là* is "there" in French, in Arabic it is "no."

"Down the street," said someone craning his neck to hear.

Another guard joined the speculation with grunts. Then a very important gentleman appeared carrying a briefcase, the guards instantly turned liquid with deference, and I remembered that here, to get ahead, it was necessary either to venerate the bureaucracy or to be fleeced by it. The gentleman hurried by, leaving the guards to gather up their bad humor. I returned to my car again. Eventually, I discovered that the minister's offices had moved to another part of town altogether.

Late as usual, I finally found him in a nineteenth-century villa that had been transformed into office space. His secretary led me to his offices. He was an extremely elegant, amiable man who had spent much time in the European capitals. I would like to have known his tailor. He was delighted to dis-

cuss Paris, and it was with some trouble that I brought the subject around to Moslem restrictions, which seemed, at the moment, to preoccupy me.

"If you want to learn about the status of women in Morocco, you must see Y and Z," he said. "Yes, surely Y and Z will be of more help than I could be. It is their field." He buzzed for his secretary. He supplied me with a staff car. He waved me on my way.

"Just remember," he said as the driver pressed his foot down on the accelerator, "veils are no indication of the depth of religious feeling."

I pondered this inside the black Mercedes, gradually becoming aware that my tennis shirt and blazer were all wrong for these high-level meetings.

Three men greeted me in a large, sprawling building surrounded by a park. They did not know quite why I was there. But the fact that X had phoned ahead was good enough reason, I suppose, since X was in a superior position. I was ushered into an office deprived of ornamentation.

"The women . . ." I began, "the position of women . . ."

They stared at me patiently.

"How can you reconcile . . . in the present era . . ." (what on earth was I doing in this office?) "and Mohammed's teaching that women are inferior to men . . ."

They jumped on that.

"The Koran makes no precise distinction."

But I knew the quote and mentioned it: "*Men have authority over women because Allah has made the one superior to the others.*"

"Less capable," said Y. "They are less physically robust, you see." He searched for another interpretation. "Less morally *impeccable.*"

He sat back in his splendid suit. The others nodded.

"There have been no female prophets," said Z.

"And as for veils," said Y, "they were instituted by the Turks under the Ottoman Empire. The Koran does not require women to veil themselves. They should be dressed from here"—he clasped his wrists—"to the ankle," and he pointed elegantly to the floor where a worn, once beautiful carpet was ending its days.

"Like *your* nuns," he added, smiling triumphantly.

Here the third man agreed. He had said nothing. I suspected that he was there because of a lunch appointment with the other two, now foreshortened by this meeting.

I looked at the three of them. They were wearing good suits and they had beautiful manners. They were comfortable and they had the right credentials. Everything they would say would be for the good of everybody.

"The rights of women have developed more quickly here in Morocco these past years," said Y, "than in France."

"In France," added Z, "women cannot have their own bank accounts, and I have heard that it is difficult also in America."

"Women can put clauses into their marriage contracts," added the other gentleman, unable, now that the subject of finance had arisen, to keep quiet. The bank account business had gotten them all talking at once.

"Property settlements are high . . ."

"The family treasurer is the *mother-in-law.*"

"The wife's possessions are under her control alone . . ."

"If the husband has not lived up to the marriage contract, it is annulled . . ."

Somewhere, the discussion had touched home. A certain energy arose as each of the gentlemen referred back to his own life. There was no further mention of female prophets.

"The woman is protected," said Y finally, "and that is as it should be."

They all hummed in acknowledgment. The goodwill made them beam. The sunlight slanting into the room touched the frame of the photograph of the King on the wall behind the desk and it glittered. The King's lips have been retouched generously: his lips are perfect. The brass fittings on

the desk glisten. There is nothing else on the desk, no fugitive scrap of paper, no rubber band. It is impeccable. They are impeccable. Their positions, their families, their women are all impeccable. I feel as though I am drowning and I wish them a good day, a perfect day, and I leave them. We have all smiled. When I get into a taxi the driver spits out of the open window and wipes his mouth on the sleeve of his heavy burnoose. My staff car has disappeared.

The Avenue Mohammed V is Rabat's main thoroughfare. It is probably the most cosmopolitan boulevard in Morocco; surely it is the swankiest. It is filled with sidewalk cafés. The strollers do not slouch and amble. Theirs is a brisk walk, heads held high, pleased by their surroundings. The few women in kaftans manage to expose their calves through clever vents in the side. Their long robes flap in the breeze; they might as well be wearing nightgowns. The men wear their hair long, and who cares if it turns to a slight frizz at the ends? Their clothes are tight, their pants seem to have no pockets, nothing is concealed. They carry handbags of leather as they do in

Rome, with the same air of narcissism. How can one object? One searches for folklore, and finding it, claims that it deprives the people of their twentieth-century rights. In a late-nineteenth-century guidebook, it is recorded that one saw:

> French soldiers and officers, Zuaves and Turcos, with their smart uniforms; the Jew, with dark colored turban, jacket and sash, blue stockings and shoes; the Moor, in smartly embroidered jacket, full short trousers, and white stockings; bare-legged Arabs wrapped in their white burnous; Mozobites, with their coats of many colors; Negroes from the Soudan; Spaniards and Maltese, all jostle one another in the crowded streets; while Moorish women, dressed in white, with full trousers, slippers, and their faces covered to the eyes, mingle with ladies in fashionable modern toilets, and with Jewesses whose jaws are bound with a muslin handkerchief, and whose straight silk robes reach from the neck to the slippered feet.

And one finds, instead, blue jeans and shiny gabardines ready to pop their seams.

Occasionally an older couple walk by. Their pace is more leisurely. They are reminiscent of an earlier era, when women in America wore Persian-lamb coats and held on to their husband's arm past rows of low neat houses on city streets (trolleys in the distance), a stately promenade. The man here wears a distinguished suit, and a turban, and rimless glasses. The woman's kaftan is of the best cloth. They are isolated, placed on the canvas by another hand from another time.

As you sit in a café watching the passing parade there is a sound at your feet as of leaves swept by a swift broom. You turn to see a boy sprawled out dragging useless limbs behind him, moving along the pavement like a wounded animal. His shaven head tilts up with a smile; one bony arm lifts from its work as a foot to make a salute which turns into an open palm to hold the coins. He drags along now to the next table of young Moroccans. The group assembled there goes on talking. One of them lights another's Marlboro with a disposable lighter. He inhales, flicks his glance down at the thing crawling next to him, fishes in his pocket (his hand alone is involved with charity) and continues his conversation. Then he tosses some money to the uplifted palm, never looking back down again at that wretchedness.

Chapter Three

MARRAKESH AND SOUTH

There is no symmetry in North Africa apart from the flawlessness of the sky above, so serene over the Sahara that you are purified by gazing at it. The countryside never rests; savage cliffs give way to gentle hills slowly drifting off to leave you alone in a barrenness of rock and shale and anxiety.

Marrakesh is set between the desolate plains of the Haouz and the foothills of the High Atlas, its snow-covered turrets holding the rest of Africa at bay. Beyond is the desert. Marrakesh is nine hundred years old and time has left it few monuments for all its years. It was created by Yusuf ibn-Tashfin, the first of the Almoravid dynasty, the strict, fanatical and highly intelligent family that ruled for a century and conquered the south. Here would rise a great city, protected by those fierce mountains, and, in turn, dominating access to them and the Sahara. A rose-red wall constructed out of the local pisé clay would encircle it. Marrakesh, from Marrokush, which became the Spanish word for the entire country: Marruecos.

Now, inside its thick walls, it is a place severely wounded. For here, exposed for all to see, is the quintessential hype and hustle of North Africa. *To some of you Allah has given more than to others*, wrote Mohammed, so that the rich might feel obliged to give to the poor. Here is the provincial axis of retribution, the commercial center-cum-resort, humming with the business of settling the accounts.

Imagine an open bazaar, the Arabian Nights you had hoped for when you began your trek east. A big, open space, the D'jmaa el Fna—the Congregation of the Dead—filled with dancers, musicians, snake charmers, fire eaters, storytellers: ah, the bliss and wonder of wandering past all this . . . this mystery and spectacle, privileged to witness the organic theater of another world. You are prodded by limbs, by whole limbs, partial limbs, limbs clothed in coarse robes and limbs smooth and naked. There is something urgent in all that prodding, now that you ponder it, and that urgency is mak-

ing it difficult for you to watch the storyteller or concentrate on the quartet of violin players and hear the Haouzia music you have understood was appreciated there. It is not the prod for elbow room that bruises you on New York's street corners. It is an attempt to get your attention, a physical prologue. You smile, at first. But your smile vanishes as you realize that the violinists have stopped playing and the cup is being passed directly to you. You take out your money too quickly, too openly; a crowd seems to begin to form around you, as though your act, too, might be worth watching. Even in the hottest months most of the other men wear many garments. Concealment is all. And only somewhere beneath the folds and pockets and layers and purses lies the person. If a man wishes to pay for something he looks to the right and to the left; then he withdraws from some secret place the leather bag containing in its many compartments the coins which, following an intricate period of self-examination and haggling, he is willing to hand over. When you carelessly pull a wallet out of your back pocket you are newly aware that all eyes in the vicinity will swivel with shameless interest in your direction and it is your lack of concealment in addition to the money exposed that dazzles them so.

"Here!" says a short dark girl, her face too old for the rest of her. She thrusts a beaded necklace into your fist, which you clench (along with your jaw, raising the muscle on your temple), now on guard.

"Take it!" she commands, standing firm on shoeless feet.

"*Imchee, seer b'halak*" Go away! You feel yourself getting harsh. You have lost the gentle course, steering now towards anger.

"It's a *gift*," she says, daring you to let go. Somehow the beaded necklace has wound itself around your wrist. This is the land of spells and potions.

"Now, listen . . ." you begin with reason. But reason is no currency. It is not good enough. You might just as well have left reason behind at the airport. She moves in closer. Others, seeing you with the necklace absurdly dangling from your wrist, come rushing over with their wares, tripping over each other. The violins start up again as a group of tourists comes into view. The new accumulation has other things to sell: uncles with carpet factories, cousins with copperware; things handwoven or things handwrought are yours for the asking. You will need a guide, you will need an interpreter, you will be brought to the souqs where water sellers will pose for their photographs and a snake charmer will charm for you alone.

"Take this necklace back," you say uselessly to the girl, who is now angrily elbowing the others away. You were hers and only hers.

"It's yours!" she shrieks. "PAY ME FOR IT!"

And you drop the necklace on the ground, released by your anger.

With rage, she snatches it up; rage and disgust. As she turns away she hurls at you the full force of her hard-won English: "Mothafuckah-sonofabitchshitbastard," and the others, seeing her defeat, take courage.

But you no longer listen. The violins now sound scratchy and irritable. Now it is you who push and shove everyone out of your way, moving fast in another direction, out of the square.

"Don't let them hassle you," says a hippie who has watched it all from the sidelines. "They've got bad vibes, man, fuck 'em."

"Do you want to fuck?" says someone alerted, running up.

And above the square of the Congregation of the Dead, a slender moon has risen, so flawless that it shocks you, stops you dead. The tall minaret of the Katoubiya, surely one of the masterpieces of the Moorish world, stands mutely staring into the calm night high above the D'jmaa el Fna. In its own past, it was given its name in the 1100's by the booksellers—the *kutubium*—who had gathered in its shadow to sell words and language to the passersby. Europe, then, was still dark. Thomas Aquinas preaching reason had not yet arrived, nor had Dante with his visions of the universe. And in America there were savages.

All over North Africa there is a certain rhythm, a long languor interrupted by a sudden abruptness. When all hope is lost at an airport, when each official has studied with slow concentration and a weary sigh each piece of camera equipment in your case, handled it, passed it around with grave permission, someone else will drift by in an equivalent uniform, presumably with an equivalent rank. Quickly he will raise one hand as though splashing cold water over his shoulder, and it is finished. You are jerked into the country with all your equipment and your luggage and someone is finding you a taxi.

Such care can be taken over details—someone arranging flowers in a bowl at teatime is still concluding the details as the sun sets—that you forget the brusqueness of someone in an automobile who just misses killing a child as he swerves around the corner and continues on his way unfazed. You watch a spice merchant sitting on a small bench in front of his spice stall thinking his thoughts. He wears a fez. A flower is tucked behind his ear. Around him are swelling sacks of curry, rosemary, beans, cumin. A pair of visitors with a camera spy him. Slowly, elegantly, he raises his index finger—his one finger indicating the one dirham it will cost them for a pose. They do not understand, or pretend not to, and, instead, they take a photograph of a man flying into a rage, advancing on them out of focus.

Marrakesh swells with this rhythm. Outside its walls, the gardens surrounding it are orderly, planted centuries ago with citrus and olive. There are reflecting pools and summer pavilions, and people sit quietly against tree trunks; here and there someone eats an orange; a child crawls noiselessly over his parents to settle into the folds of their robes. Insect sounds, bird sounds, and the rest is quiet. The frenzy of the Medina, the Mellah and the D'jmaa el Fna are forgotten. Foreigners who live in Marrakesh remain at home around courtyards and fountains, the jungle of crowded streets pressing against their high, unperturbed walls.

It is a strange choice for the international set. It is not next to the sea, nor is it set in a mountain; during the winter it is not quite warm enough and in the summer the African sun scorches everything in sight after ten in the morning. But it is the closest place to Europe, offering the sense of a tamed other world—a kind of painless exoticism. There is just enough hazard, just enough beauty and squalor and just enough safety. The newest hotel abuts the D'jmaa el Fna. Its wall is so high and so complete, and its front door is so discreetly—or cautiously—placed, that the building seems to be pretending not to be there at all—which is in perfect accord with the Arab sensibility. The Mamounia, however, the grand and luxurious Mamounia, is aloof from all the helter-skelter of the center of town, backed up against an orange grove just before the town's rose-red wall. I understand that it is being westernized and modernized, those insatiable twins that eventually attack all things combining history and commerce. The lobby is so vast that it could accommodate a herd of elephants, and at cocktail time the costumed waiters, the multinational clientele, the piano music morbidly resounding throughout the various public rooms and corridors give the effect of a great liner permanently beached, its true destination long forgotten.

"What happened to John?" I asked the girl lying next to me on her striped mattress at the Mamounia's pool, her bathing paraphernalia bereft of the designer's symbols announcing the other guests' territory.

She propped herself up on her shoulders to study me.

"The railroad station in Tangier," I said. "I saw you both carted off."

"Oh, *for God's sake!*" she cried, sitting upright, throwing her arms up in the air as though we were long-lost friends. I had remembered her face and her bottom but I had forgotten her emphasis.

"He was sent packing to London. Well, it's been absolutely *ghastly!*"

"Being alone," I said.

"I mean, traveling without a man. And not for the reasons that you think. I can't go anywhere! I can't look at anything! I came here to see the East. Like that groupie what's-her-name who hung on to Sir Richard Burton. Oh, *not* Elizabeth," she said, looking pained.

"Lady Isabel," I suggested.

"That's it! Lady Isabel Burton! Following caravans. Long, flowing robes. That kind of thing."

"Your costume at the station," I said, "was, ah, much briefer."

"But not *now!* Not now that I'm *alone!* I've been going around with a skirt down to my bloody ankles. I've tied my hair in a kerchief—they're kinky about blond hair. None of it's any use. My trip's almost over and I've spent most of my time around this boring *pool!*"

A waiter came over to take an order for drinks. He glanced at us with pro-

fessional indifference and left. His babouches—slippers without backs or heels—clopped along the tiles.

"You see!" she trilled. *"He's* not the slightest bit interested in me. As long as you're at an hotel you're not a peculiarity. But as soon as you walk in their streets they go absolutely *dotty."*

I applied some suntan oil to her back. "It can't be all that bad," I said.

"I took one ride on a camel," she said in a smaller voice. "It was with a group of elderly ladies from the hotel. I have a photograph of it. I mean," she continued, getting back her enthusiasm, "I'd adore it if it were admira*tion.* But their treatment of women is an *ill*ness. It's a national epidemic!"

Orthodox Moslems believe that ideally a woman should go out only three times in her life: when she leaves her mother's womb, when she leaves her father's house to marry, and when she leaves life once and for all in a pine box carried on the shoulders of the men in her family. Women glide by in the streets often accompanied by a muffled jingling sound, a sound that seems to come through heavily curtained rooms. These are the keys they carry on their person—and everything in the Arab world is kept under lock and key—close to their anatomy: something that seals hidden behind some-

thing disguised. They move briskly, pursued by an invisible masculine ill will. When they are immobile, they blend into the scenery. A segment in a stack of pottery or a sack of laundry will slowly disassemble itself from the area surrounding it and walk away, an object in motion. It strolls, it stoops; then it squats, haggles, purchases, carries, stops, gossips, turns and vanishes.

Alone in the house, women remove the litham—the veil covering most of the face—and their long outer robe, the haik, to move freely within their walls or on the rooftops. Gathering in their rooms to drink glasses of mint tea, to gossip or to dance for each other, they await the convulsive moment when the presence of the male is noted mounting the stairs or entering an adjoining room. Immediately the guests slip into their concealing garments to drift out of the house as though they were made of air.

So much of the interior world is dominated by concealment and reticence that the American need to reveal and communicate begins to seem, after a while, like something dreamed. In America we are urged to exhibit ourselves, *tell it like it is, let it all hang out.* Our waitresses wearing nameplates call us honey; so do our conventioneers. We attend encounter sessions stark naked with strangers, and, naked too, we plunge into pools and out of cakes. SMILE, it says in shopwindows. TRY GOD, it says on vermeil pins. HONK IF YOU LOVE JESUS, it says on bumper stickers. So we publicly smile, we stroke, we plunge, pop and honk. And to an Arab meditating in his voluminous shrouds, we are lunatics.

Zeus imposed upon Atlas the punishment of carrying the sky on his shoulders. It is a strange choice for heaven's support, this mountain in Morocco named in his honor, with a height less than half that of Kilimanjaro, more in league with Colorado's Lookout Peak. But its savagery might have appealed to the Greeks. Few low mountain chains seem as wild as this. The villages remain apart from the rest of the country, high on the cliffs, closer, you might say, to heaven. Their architecture is fixed at some eternal level— the earth color of the walls, and the delicate tracery of the rooftops. Storks nest high in the crenelations. It is a land of eyries. The landscape takes on a mythical significance all the way to the sea.

The magic practiced in Morocco has filtered down from here. In the towns and villages there are stalls in the souqs providing philters and powders and arsenic. Bat's wings and heron's skulls; feathers of this and dung from that are available to housewives wanting revenge, needing to settle the accounts. Strange preparations are created and administered in secret. The husbands never know what magic is waiting in store for them. Does a fish know, when a pelican comes towards it from out of the sky, smiling, its shadow slowly shrinking, what that opened beak and empty pouch portend?

There are laws against the practice of magic. But when skin mottles, hair falls out, or there is a slow, almost imperceptible decline into derangement, who can prove the causes? It is said that the least attractive girl in town with the best connection in sorcery can arrange to bring into matrimony the most appealing bachelor in the neighborhood—vague, but still mobile. Berber ladies tattoo their thighs and abdomen when they marry, hoping to attract fertile spirits. Widows are allowed, up to five years following the death of their husbands, to bear *children of the bier*. The child is supposed to have been asleep in the womb. And they throw boiling water into the sinks to discourage evil spirits from emerging into the household through the plumbing.

In 1960, on a winter day, an earthquake demolished almost all of Agadir, a seacoast town in southern Morocco. Fifteen thousand people died in fifteen seconds. Only memories of the place remained. For many years after, long rows of men from the surrounding countryside worked along the beaches with pickaxes and shovels, clearing the cement and rock and debris imbedded in the sand. Along the port in the late afternoons, fishing boats continued to arrive piled high with the sardines that had once brought some prosperity to the town. Young boys filled the cranes with the fish, climbing onto the cranes themselves, their own bodies coated in the opalescent fish scales, and they would be lifted high above the docks, glistening. Then the docks and the workers grew lavender, and the sand and the hills beyond the ruined citadel, and the sharp remnants of what was left of Agadir were outlined against the evening sky.

The beaches were empty. I was alone in Agadir after the earthquake. So insubstantial was the city that my stay there took on the quality of a faulty hallucination. The reality of the new construction would intrude upon the vast stretches of phantom shapes still standing in ruins. I wandered along the deserted sand. The sky frequently turned grey, and strong winds rose from the west, chopping the sea into tight ridges. One day, feeling restless, I walked far from the town to the distant sand dunes finding a calm place to take the sun, listening to the wind over my head. The day had grown extremely hot. I was anxious to leave Agadir, and because I had arranged to take a bus the following day, I could no longer sit still or concentrate on anything. Part of me, I suppose, had already left. I ran down the face of the dune to dive into the ocean and when I came back I found that my towel had slid to the back of the dune into the eucalyptus below. The sun had begun to burn through the haze. I walked cautiously to retrieve the towel, the dead eucalyptus leaves crackling underfoot. When I kneeled to pick up the towel I saw a young Arab sitting at the base of one of the lean trees.

In his hand was a knife. He carefully sharpened the stalk of a palm frond and looked over at me with a half-smile. Did I remember him, he asked, from the sardine boats? A face twice seen in this country is an acquaintance. I said, yes, that I knew the boats, and that it must be fun to ride the cranes way up above the docks. Then I asked what he was doing with the knife.

"For fun," he said, *pour m'amuser*. He took careful aim, throwing the sharpened stalk to pierce a leaf on the sand.

I nodded, and then I smiled.

He slid the knife into the top of his bathing suit and slowly walked over to a bicycle propped against the trees. He asked me whether I smoked kif.

I said that sometimes I did, and I watched him carefully unwrap a bag strapped to the bike. He took out an orange and then peeled it with great care using his knife, coming over to me to hold it up to my mouth. It was warm and bitter. Then he lit a reed pipe and passed it to me. I stretched out on the sand, inhaling the kif and looking at the dune. He filled the pipe again, concentrating on it. His face was very young, its features incompletely formed, not caught up with his body. When he came back with the pipe, he studied me, put the pipe aside; then he abruptly crouched over me. I had sensed it was coming, preparing myself to spring. The dead leaves were now in sharp relief near my face, the sun beating down as we struggled and turned, moving now in an easier way, almost gentle. "*Let me*," he said, and with his hands he held very tightly to my wrists. He brought his forehead down to touch mine; his pale brown eyes seemed to join into one eye. "*Let me*," he said again. I moved my face from side to side, his face turning with me, sliding, both of us covered with sweat. He lifted his hands to my shoulders. "Then you can have me later," he said, his lips brushing my ear. I could find no voice. And in the moment, through the trees, I saw a figure standing, wearing a khaki uniform. A violence seized me and in one motion I stood.

The Arab saw it at the same time. He lifted himself from the sand in anger, brushing the sand from his shoulders as he went over to the man in uniform in the woods. Quickly I looked for the knife, and not finding it, I started back towards the dunes.

"No, it's all right," he said, running over to me. "He's the guardian here. There are two of them. They'll go away. Then they want to come back," he said, lowering his voice, "to be with you."

I started to talk in English. The words made no sense, the change of language surprising him, and he looked to the other Arab as though trying with his help to puzzle out this strangeness. With the torpor found in dreams, I climbed the dunes, my feet digging into the sand flowing back to cover them.

From the crest above, I could feel the wind from the sea, and then I turned back. Three figures stood in the clearing. From above, the sweep of eucalyptus seemed to go on forever. The boy looked up at me shaking his fist. "You have brought dishonor to yourself to have run away," he shouted.

Then he pounded his hand against his chest. "And me," he called, "you have brought me dishonor not to have stayed with me."

It was a long walk back along the sand.

I will write in this narrative of the richest country and the richest man in the world. These are their legends, although I find such superlatives worrying. But it would seem unfair not to include the richest woman; that is, the woman who bore the title, because she, too, passed my way in the Moslem world. The woman, Barbara Hutton, was staying at a hotel set in a twenty-acre park not far from Taroudant, a rust-red town an angrier shade and further south than Marrakesh. It is surrounded by high walls and cramped lanes, and there is sand beyond its oases. On the grounds of the hotel there was a pool; camels grazed on the lawns; each guest had his own cottage filled with fresh flowers and stacks of olive wood for its fire-

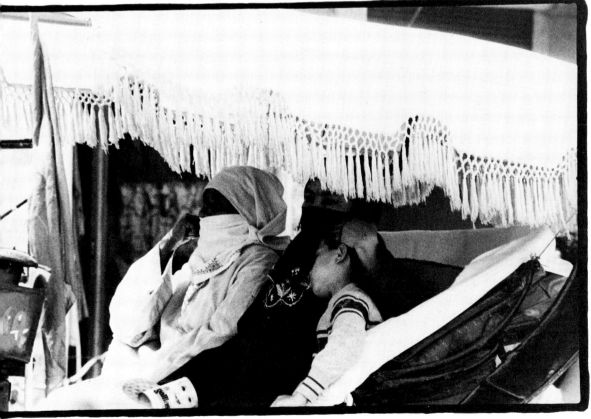

places. It was an enchanted place connected not at all to the ferment of the town beyond.

It was to this hotel that I was heading in the back seat of a car. An elephant-grey Rolls-Royce raises a lot of dust in Morocco. Thundering like a faraway storm, the automobile brushed fowl aside, mildly interested the camels along the plains and streaked past the robed figures at the side of the road who followed it with shaded eyes, mistrustfully. Finally it crunched to a stop on the gravel just in time for tea.

Our hostess was frail. Her patrician good looks were marked by some muffled distress, masked, because of careful breeding, as mild exasperation. At odd moments, she would unexpectedly pull rank, emboldened by her own legend, demanding the tiresome kind of homage extracted by most celebrated people. She had had husbands and houses and jewelry in great quantities, several lifetimes' worth, but her delicate, somewhat frightened manner suggested that these were but earthly ornaments decorating a life lived elsewhere, on an ethereal plane untouched by men and stones.

At each period of the day she wore a different complement of jewelry, replenishing the myth: now rubies, now turquoise, now jade. It was jade at tea. She sat in front of a tall window, a Vermeer light touching her profile, the surfaces of the wood and the jewels. The jade obliged the sunlight with a leafy translucence. Her husband stopped at her chair to ask what she might want from town. Slippers, she said, turning away, and she stayed behind with her teacup and her jewelry underneath the long window with the light falling soothingly on the surfaces.

In proper Arabian Nights fashion, there was to be a banquet. It was the autumn. I remember this because she and I were the only Americans there, and it was decided that Thanksgiving was to be celebrated. The town was searched for turkeys, but none were to be found. Instead, chickens were brought—spare birds, having pecked at the bone-dry earth of Africa, would now end their days disguised as another fowl for a holiday unknown to anyone but us. The walls of the dining room were covered in a deep red; there were candles and flowers and crystal goblets and the grapefruit had been fashioned into baskets, waiting, as were the assembled guests, for the tardy arrival of the hostess. The candlelight wove flapping shadows around the darkened room.

> *Think, in this battered Caravansary*
> *Whose portals are alternate Night and Day,*
> *How Sultan after Sultan with his pomp*
> *Abode his destined hour and went his way.**

* *The Rubáiyát of Omar Khayyám*, Verse 17 (New York: Grosset & Dunlap, Inc., 1946). Used by permission of Grosset & Dunlap, Inc.

And all at once she appeared at the top of the staircase, flanked on either side by her Oriental husband and his brother—her Mandarins—each wearing kaftans brocaded in gold and silver. Frail between them, motionless in a gown with sleeves touching the floor, she shimmered with jewels. Suspended from her ears, around her wrists, circling her fingers, were diamonds like constellations. Around her neck in tier after tier was the emerald necklace that Catherine the Great had worn ruling Russia.

"Good heavens!" said our hostess with surprise from the top of the staircase, her hand flying to her neck. "What are you all gaping at?"

Africa could contain this shred of the fanciful without effort. This is the land of storytellers and visionaries and dream-haunted tales. In the south of Morocco, there are jinnis behind the rocks, hiding in the hills, until all of it ends, cleansed by the purity of the Sahara. TIMBUCTOO, says a sign at the great desert's edge, FIFTY-TWO DAYS BY CAMEL. A prankish note, the last of the signs. No footsteps begin here, no caravan to cross it, no further way into Africa. And no possibility of looking out at that mighty desert without resolving to see what was on its other side.

Chapter Four

ACROSS THE SAHARA

We flew over Mauritania, high above the Sahara, stopping only briefly at Nouahibou. There was sand everywhere, sand as far as the eye could see. But not the sand you might like to imagine, not the rolling dunes, the sand that lured Lawrence. This was rough sand in low ridges, sand like gravel covering the bottom of a fish tank waiting to be submerged, planted, waiting for signs of life. The sandstorms blow all night, bringing a glacial chill from the low desert into the towns. Then in the mornings the streets are swept, the sand is pushed back so that people can walk and jeeps can pass. The next morning it is the same, and the next: sand held at bay. It seems the towns would go under and be gone if everyone were to stop sweeping. There is iron and copper in Mauritania, and tons of dried fish are sent from its shores. The Mauritanians—there are about a million—are considered to be very hospitable and extremely religious. Sometimes they give in to the temptation and lie down in the barren, treeless land, letting the sun and sand do what it will.

On the plane, my neighbor was a young black gentleman wearing a long, flowing white robe, and next to him sat his even younger wife. On her lap sprawled their baby.

"I have come from Mecca," he said. "I've made my hadj, my pilgrimage. I also managed to do a little business there. Everyone does."

"The people from Mecca in particular," I said, "or so I understand."

"They do very well, very well indeed. Every *centimeter* of their property is rented out to pilgrims. They come by the millions. A plane every two minutes. It is so crowded that families lose each other." He reached over to pat his wife and baby. "And some of the old ones never return."

On his lap, he carried a large aluminum jug of water, and tied to it was a great metal teapot. On the planes to Mecca it is not unknown that a passenger will begin to prepare tea by building a small wood fire in the aisles, quickly extinguished by the wild-eyed stewardesses.

When the baby began to cry on his wife's lap, he picked it up absently.

"Here," he said, "take this," handing the baby over to me.

Staring up at me with astonishment, the baby stopped crying. I patted it. It hiccupped. Lunch was served and it went to sleep under my hinged tray.

"What's this?" inquired the Senegalese, pointing to the smoked salmon. It seemed an odd thing to serve above the Sahara. I told him what it was.

"And how is it eaten?"

"On toast. Except in America, where they seem to prefer it on a bagel."

He turned to his wife to report these facts. She looked at me dubiously. Then she tucked herself inside her shawls and veils and napped.

"And this?" he asked, fingering a foil-covered napkin on his tray.

"Don't eat that," I said quickly.

The baby began to cry as the lunch trays were taken away. The mother roused herself and unfolded a beautiful breast to it.

"These customs forms," said the Senegalese with a confidence that seemed characteristic. "You will fill them out for me." He then handed me his passport, his wife and baby's passport and the forms. His wife, I noticed on the passport, was fifteen. I dutifully transferred the information onto the forms, showed him where to sign and was gently tapped on the shoulder by a man behind me who smiled, and wordlessly handed me his passport, his forms. Then he nodded encouragingly, and I nodded back, glancing apprehensively as other passports, other forms came my way. Below us, the desert gaped obtusely at the sky.

"You do it so quickly," said the young Moroccan across the aisle. "The ability to write, in these countries, is limited to the few." He swept his open palm to include the plane and the cloudless sky. "I know. I conduct surveys. In Mauritania there are only forty thousand students. And there are a million camels."

I continued my transcriptions.

"What do you do?" the Moroccan inquired of the Senegalese next to me.

"I work for Allah," replied the Senegalese. On his passport I had noted that his occupation was listed as *ouvrier spécial*, which seemed reasonable.

"I mean, to earn money," persisted the Moroccan.

He brushed the question aside. "Allah requires no money. Allah provides," he said, tilting his chair back with satisfaction.

"He does not provide everything," sighed the Moroccan. "Even to those of us who are truly religious."

"What do you lack?" asked the Senegalese before dozing off.

"Women," answered the Moroccan urgently, brushing some lint from the lapel of his jacket.

Jesus, again, I said under my breath.

The Senegalese slumbered.

"I have a fiancée," continued the Moroccan, addressing himself now to me. "But our religion forbids us to sleep with each other. And I do not like whores or boys. I like only nice, *sortable* ladies," he said primly, still brushing his now spotless lapel.

"When will you get married?" I asked politely.

"In four or five years. When I can afford it. By then I will be close to thirty."

"And meanwhile?" I asked absently.

"I masturbate," he said, sighing. "It is a smaller sin."

An attack of claustrophobia overtook me; the plane, the restrictions of Islam, its obsessions. I shut my eyes. When I awoke, we were about to land.

"You will help us with our baggage," said the Senegalese, gathering together various baskets, boxes, thermoses, his wife, the teapot and the baby.

"No," I said. "No, I won't."

And we were on the ground.

North of the Sahara, in Morocco, you bake in the heat and complain. To the Sahara's south, you boil. Baking is preferable. Eventually you turn to a crisp, still composed cinder. But boiling is a liquid business. Seams give way and you feel yourself begin to squash.

In the baggage area I met a French industrialist in the process of trying to move a crazed dog in a large cage from one gaggle of officials to another. The dog had made the cross-Saharan trip in the bowels of the plane, and according to the customs men it did not now have the look of a reputable alien. There were serious conferences about it and, to its dismay, the dog's tongue now hung down to its toes. The Frenchman rapidly cut through all the red tape with an imperious harangue that would have made any colonialist proud. They released the dog after some bills changed hands. When I brought the dog a paper cup of water the Frenchman suggested that he help get me a room in an air-conditioned hotel. Outside the airport we were immediately surrounded by kids asking us for money.

"Want, want, want!" stormed the Frenchman. "That's all you hear in Africa. *Here!*" he said, thrusting at the ragged band the filthy blanket he had extracted from the dog's cage, which he then collapsed, heaving it into the trunk of a taxi. "Now let's get out of here."

We slammed the door of the car and the dog lay at our feet in an extended state of dementia.

"You will hate Dakar," said my new acquaintance.

"Thanks," I said. "Just the right thing to hear on my way into town."

He looked surprised. His bright blue eyes scanned me briefly; then he glanced out of the window.

"They are stupid here. Keep that always in mind. My wife and I had a servant who cooked for us whose specialty was *tomates farcies*. We were famous for it when we entertained. Everyone wanted the recipe. A few weeks ago my wife went into the kitchen while the servant was preparing the dish. She found him *chewing the meat,* and then stuffing the tomatoes with it. Remember that. And there was a perfectly good meat grinder I brought back from Paris."

I patted the dog, whose eyes, like mine, were rolling dangerously back into his forehead.

"And also," continued my chum, "quite frankly, they have an unpleasant odor when they perspire."

"Now, *look . . .*" I began angrily.

"Spare me a discussion on racism," he interrupted. "I know almost everything you're going to say. I said it all when I first came here from France." He fanned himself with his passport. The dog breathed heavily, then he panted, then he gulped. I pushed the cup of water over to him and he knocked it over with his nose. My back had become glued to the car's upholstery. My shoes were now wet. I tried to look out of the open window and sweat ran into my lashes. The Frenchman was expounding on the Africans' lack of manners. *"C'est moche,"* he repeated. *"Oh, que c'est moche!"* His passport clicked back and forth circulating the hot air near my ear. *"C'est dé-gueu-lasse!"*

"You see those new buildings?" he asked suddenly. We were now in the center of the city. The main square was ringed with skyscrapers.

"Only for the rich!" he exclaimed. "The poor are given nothing."

"Where are your offices?" I asked.

"That has nothing to do with it," he snapped. Then he directed the driver to take a shortcut to the hotel. I was aware of brightly colored clothes on a street with some shade, and we had arrived. A man rushed over to the car to sell fake gold nuggets secreted in a Kleenex. Someone else sidled by with a carved wooden statuette remarkable for the size of its lips. The Frenchman ordered them away sharply and they obediently disappeared into the meager shadows.

But to his credit, he did arrange—above the objections of the room clerk, who insisted that none was available—to get me a room. I was to run into the Frenchman only once again, which I considered an additional piece of good fortune. And I am pleased to report that the dog managed as we said our goodbyes to lift his leg against a tree and relieve himself. I thought I heard him sigh. He was relieving himself still as I finally got myself and my baggage out of the taxi and into the hotel.

Senegal's story is a classic West African tale. Until late in the seventeenth century it was of no interest to the rest of the world. Hot places were to be avoided; there were fearsome natives, there were strange illnesses and no cures, and there was not nearly enough drinkable water to go around. The

search for gold and ivory finally made the interior of the continent more interesting to the great colonial powers not yet thinking about oil. Dakar is
the closest point in Africa to South America, and the Ile Gorée—just off the
coast—was used by the Dutch as a commercial port. Inevitably the slave
trade began. Africans made good ballast for empty ships returning to South
America. Villages were burned, the natives were caught fleeing the flames,
their captors aided, of course, by the local chieftains. Then they were sent
to Gorée to await their boats. Their shipping house still stands. One stark
door opens onto the shiny rocks; then there is the sheet of sea stretching to
South America. The slaves were stored in cubicles in this house (it is a
smudged pink)—stored and sized and sexed—and through this doorway they
left Africa forever.

Shipwrecks became a thriving business along the African coastline. Anyone owning a piece of the shore could claim a wreck off it as their property.
Ships followed lights misleading them to boulders. Before they foundered
and sank, their crews were ransomed and their cargo was seized. It was to
eliminate this problem—with one eye on Dakar's good military position
along the coastline—that the French decided to take it over. It is one of the

most cheerful stories of an occupation yet recorded, occurring, coincidentally, in the period of Gilbert and Sullivan.

A warship called the *Jeanne d'Arc* carrying French sailors enters the African harbor in the spring of 1857. The Moslem natives are celebrating the end of the long fasting of Ramadan. Wearing their jaunty uniforms, the visitors come ashore. They are included in the celebration. The ship's captain (with the genial name of Protet) hands the French tricolor to the local chieftains, who pass it around admiringly. Then it is hoisted above the town, fluttering red, white and blue in the breeze. The following day it is still there, and so are the French. And there they remained.

When it became a territory there were only fifteen hundred natives. By 1940, when Dakar was an important shipping center and naval base, the population had reached seventy-five thousand. Now it is a city scrambled together with over a half million. This sudden population has only increased the aura of musical comedy. The place has an air of madness, as though some spacy director-in-the-sky had inherited a town, some building blocks, an incredible range of flesh-tone pigments and endless yards of bright batik to costume his characters. The array of races is itself astonishing, more wonderful even than the range of garments they wear. The names: the Ouolofs, the darkest people in Africa, who have given Senegal (and Gambia) its language. They are Moslems, often unusually tall, and bold. There are Mandingos, Bambaras, and there are the Fulbes—the wanderers from the East—their name meaning "scattered" in their own language. Their features are frequently as refined as those of the ancient Egyptians. There are the Fulas, a combination of Negroes and Fulbes, and the Lebus—the Berbers—and the Dojhendem (*dojh*, march, and *endem*, go away), the nomads. Finally there are the Toucouleurs, just as their name suggests, a mixture of African races who themselves have become a race.

I stood dazed on the street. Shimmering governmental Mercedes' swerved around corners where tribal individuals just in from the savannah stood shoeless. How long ago did the passengers leaning against that tufted upholstery arrive on those corners? A tall woman walked past me balancing a mammoth fish on top of her head, wrapped high in a purple turban with an orange pattern of pineapples; the long *boubou* she wore was crimson embroidered with pink. She was magnificent.

I was on my way to see a minister. My previous dealings with ministers in Morocco were not, as you might have noted, triumphs. But that morning I had looked carefully at my finances. Normally I will do anything to avoid such an investigation, but something had alerted me. I think it was the price of a glass of orange juice. I realized in a terrible moment of clarity that I would manage to stay in Senegal the required week of my ticket only if I sat very still, without perspiring too much, ate almost nothing, and then, hav-

ing paid the spectacular hotel bill, I might leave. I had not bothered to inform myself that this random port on the Atlantic is, in the tradition of these superlatives, the second most expensive city in the world.

I had been told in New York that the Minister would do *everything in his power* so that I might get to know Senegal. I would need only to ask. The President of the country was, after all, a poet, greatly respected. I would be *chez moi*. No need to worry about such details as money. Now I had gone once again through my traveler's checks, rubbing their corners as I turned them, hoping for that exhilarating disjunction of two stuck pages separating. But the paper would yield nothing further. It was a thin checkbook that I tossed into the drawer before calling the Minister from the precious coolness of my room. The Minister was out. I was asked to call back. I called back. The Minister could not be located. My credentials rang no bell. I decided to pay him a call.

DÉLÉGATION GÉNÉRALE AU TOURISME, it said on a sign. Inside the vestibule a lone plant was dying in a box of caked earth.

"The Minister?" I asked, peering in through a half-opened door. It was a mail room. Two Senegalese, heads together, were guffawing at the contents of an envelope.

"Upstairs," they said in unison. "No, not that door, that's the bathroom."

Upstairs, I asked again. "The Minister?" A young lady sat at a desk reading a magazine. She tilted her head to one side, and considering the heat it was remarkable that she bothered to smile. I felt encouraged. She told me that she was his secretary. I introduced myself.

"Oh, *you*," she asked. "I told him you called."

"I see."

"He's on vacation."

"Which," I said, "is why he doesn't answer his messages."

"He gets his messages," she said. "He stops by every day and picks them up."

"Keeps them from accumulating."

"The reason I always ask you to call back is that you might catch him while he's here picking up his messages."

"He was going to do *everything in his power*," I said lamely.

"Yes," she said.

"Yes," said I.

"Maybe you can wait until his vacation is over. It only lasts another month."

"That won't be too convenient."

"I see," she said. "I'd give you a tourist brochure but the office is closed."

"Don't trouble."

"No," she said, glancing at her open magazine.

You sense the Islamic presence in the streets, particularly at dusk when, in a doorway or on the sidewalk, someone will meticulously open a straw mat and, facing East, kneel in prayer. Eighty-five percent of the country is Moslem, and yet the Arabs are regarded with caution. The President of the country is a Roman Catholic, and his concept of *Négritude* is of a separate cultural base linking all black people. The Arabs spread Islam below the Sahara in the eleventh century, even before the founding of Marrakesh. Further south, towards the equator, the unfathomable animistic religions begin. The Senegalese have taken the essence of the Moslems—a fatalism as pure as the desert—fusing it with the worship of spirits. They carry charms, and symbols; strange superstitions punctuate their logic. But the energy ebbs and flows as it does in Islamic North Africa: a sudden sulk, a removal, a rag-doll passivity abruptly stops the frenetic activity.

Along the streets leading into the market, stall keepers in bright colors stare into space, chewing methodically on *cure-dents*, the sticks used to polish their teeth into an enviable whiteness no toothbrush could ever achieve. Then there is a crowd at the next booth, the vendor is all briskness and chatter. Everyone jockeys for position to touch and gape at his wares, shouting for the bargain, shouting for encouragement, shouting just to shout. Hands are shaken in a Harlem slap of palm on palm, quickly followed by an Islamic investigation of everyone's state of health and the health of their families. No one really listens until something startling is revealed; then eyes pop tribally: pop and roll; big grins spread like sheets flapping in the moonlight. The laughter is from way inside. On the buses everyone talks to everyone else and touches each other for emphasis. It is not like the London Underground, where the passengers sit ruefully, each looking as though he has just lost a parent. Here, if there is something to say, it is aired then and there. With only a few melons you can set up shop on the pavement and enter the world of commerce. You are entitled to open conversations, salute old friends, draw crowds if you have a mind to. You are in the mainstream.

"*Chef*," someone called to me. "Is it true that the American astronauts found positive proof on the moon that God exists, and that He is Allah, and that there will be a mass movement to Islam?"

The short, animated man addressing me was surrounded by bolts of cotton. He was perched on a stool behind the counter and whisked flies away as he talked, with a tail feather of some tropical bird.

"Not that I'd heard," I said, "but there's an awful lot that I haven't heard."

"I read it," he said, leaning over to smooth a piece of batik folded in front of him. "Oh, don't feel as though you have to buy anything. This isn't my stall. It belongs to a cousin."

"You're the first person in Africa who's said that to me. I don't know whether your cousin would approve."

He shrugged, "I don't have a commercial mind. I like music. I've got

records"—he drew the feather up above his head—"stacked that high." Then he told me his name, asked me mine, went through the whole obligatory rigamarole about the states of our health and well-being while the feather resumed flicking away the flies. When I told him where I was staying, he hopped off his stool, landed on his very short feet and told me I was crazy.

"Rip-off. That's my latest word. I will try to use it twice today. Go to this hotel . . ." He scribbled something on a piece of wrapping paper, handed it to me, picked up the long feather and resumed his post on the stool. "The man who runs it is a friend. A nice guy. Mention my name. *Il ne va pas vous rip-offer.*" He chuckled. Then he leaned back, facing the bolts of cotton, and sang:

> "Put on your hi heel sneakers,
> 'Cause we're goin' out tonight.
> Put on your hi heel sneakers,
> 'Cause we're goin' out tonight,
> You better wear some boxing gloves, yeah
> In case some fool might wanna fight . . ."

"Pretty good, eh?" he asked, swiveling around to imagine applause.

I told him that it certainly was, took the paper, thanked him and went my way.

It worked like a charm. That evening I moved into the one air-conditioned room of a second-floor hotel run by the nice guy. The air conditioner coughed and sputtered and began to blow tepid air into my room in the middle of the night. Then, abruptly, its gears locked, metal ground against metal as it grew steadily warmer, something flew out of it, landing with a dull thud against the wall, and it stopped. The following day it was removed. The rectangular opening in the wall remained, open to the air, becoming a hard-edged lithograph of sky, a margin of corrugated rooftops and the very top of a palm tree. This picture would constantly alter its colors throughout the day until it went black and new forms would appear, a light show, now, of African constellations and an African moon.

Voices in the corridor throughout the night and day quickly announced that this was not an ordinary hotel, but something more resembling a *hôtel du passage*. Doors opened and closed too frequently for normal use; there was good-natured laughter in the halls, and occasionally the sound of passion or its equivalent could be distinguished. Since I had been given the deluxe accommodations—the room with the air conditioner—I had the sensation after several days that I was some family retainer still around from an earlier, less profligate era.

The owner of the place was a cheerful, stocky Frenchman whose past included the spectacular ups and downs only to be found in émigrés to the darker parts of Africa. Here a hotel, there a mine, now some commerce, now some trafficking, then some trouble with the authorities. And always the ability to start again on some scheme with a small cache of current belongings, a few pals in influential places and a current passport. His name was Le Mouleau, and he wore on his small, stocky finger a gold ring with a crest that may or may not have belonged to his family. We became immediate friends.

Le Mouleau would preside at teatime, assembling around him an appropriately eclectic group from Dakar's bohemian gentry and several folks who wandered in, like myself, just passing through. The walls of the small reception room were the color attributed to flamingos, and a fanciful oil of flamingos themselves, in balletic poses, hung slightly off balance on the wall. Several tables covered with plastic cloths were decorated with small bud vases of lean plastic daisies (the tables were never set; the daisies were never dusted); a plant with fleshy leaves leaned towards the window trying to peer down at the courtyard below, where one lone palm held court to the laundry. The quantity of laundry was impressive, occupying two laundresses, one big and hearty and the other thin and morose, one who bustled and one who shambled, the bustler scrubbing and the shambler ironing, and occasionally they would collide in the corridor. Over everything, over the reception room, the hotel, the streets, and over Dakar itself hung the strong heavy odor of peanuts. Like the sound of music in recent skyscrapers, it was unavoidable. Mountains of peanuts would pile up in the mind's eye throughout the day and night. The peanut industry, it is quickly learned, is the major resource in the country.

Le Mouleau would sometimes go into his rooms and extract, from a safe concealed behind a false cabinet, certain mementos of his elaborate past. The photograph album was his favorite, and he would entertain me with family anecdotes as he pointed to the yellowing pictures, the album spilling shreds of dry black paper over everything. "We never went hungry," he would say after showing me the private park that surrounded the family home outside of Paris. Then the book would be closed and he would stand, scattering the paper fragments from his lap with quick fingers like a fatigued emperor dismissing his court.

Champagne sometimes took the place of tea in his pink reception room. Long crystal goblets would appear, carefully carried through the many borders that formed his past. It was a brave, comedy ceremony. Le Mouleau slowly raised the cork, we of the ragtag assembly would collectively inhale until it popped and then we made sounds of satisfaction, as he swiftly brought the bottle to the lineup of crystal goblets set out on the plastic cloths (the dusty daisy wreathed in a smile); upstairs the comings and goings through the hallway scratched along the ceiling, and the odor of peanuts drifted in through the open window to embrace us all.

"That palm tree in the garden," said an elderly Frenchwoman, turning to me, "it was here forty years ago, surrounded by sand. I remember it well. Dakar was empty. One could walk down the street and not see a soul. One day I took a walk, and the only other person to pass, holding an umbrella against the sun, was the lawyer.

"My husband, who built most of the buildings here, was respected. He would get up at a construction site with a—what do you call those things?" She turned the hand not holding the glass of champagne into a horn which grew wider as she fanned out her fingers.

"A megaphone?" I suggested.

"Exactly. A megaphone. He would get up with his megaphone and shout to the men: 'Do it *this* way! Get moving!'" She paused and looked out of the window once again at the palm tree. "It would become a kind of chant. They moved with it. They built the buildings that way, respecting him."

"Ouolof wasn't spoken then," said an angular man I understood to be a painter.

"I know," said the Frenchwoman. "After independence everyone learned it. But I was already too old."

"*Voilà!*" said a woman in a red boubou who worked on television. She

drew the word out, stretching it in imitation of the French; voo-ah-*laah*.
"It's always the same with the *colons*. They never bother with the local language. They're never interested enough. We were just a bunch of niggers to
be exploited. Now, don't take it personally," she added, tapping the older
woman with her long fingers.

The woman said that she certainly wouldn't, and looked again out at the
tree.

"Well, we *were!*" said the painter. "In some ways we still are."

The woman from television withdrew her hand to her breast in horror.

"If you ladies will forgive me—you are both women of the world," said
the painter. "Last month, my mother decided that my daughter should be
circumcised."

"Your daughter!" asked the Frenchwoman despite herself.

"You see!" said the other woman. "You people don't even know what
goes on here."

"I hadn't meant to get into biology," said the painter.

"Then don't," said Le Mouleau.

"That's perfectly all right," said the elderly Frenchwoman, taking a genteel sip of champagne. "As you said, I'm a woman of the world. I think I'll
have one of your cigarettes," she whispered to me.

"Well, anyway, my mother—not my wife, mind you, but my mother—
insists that it's necessary so that later, when she grows up and gets married,
she'll remain faithful to her husband. If she finds no pleasure in making
love, why look for another man?"

"To find some pleasure from him," said Le Mouleau, shifting in his chair.
"And if not from him, from someone else. There's no end to looking for
pleasure when you don't have it." He grunted, setting down his glass.

"My point exactly," said the painter. "Sheer Islamic barbarism. I've con-
vinced my mother, I think."

"What about your wife?" asked the younger woman, leaning forward
aggressively. "Doesn't she have any say about it?"

"My mother runs the house. My wife is of two minds."

"A perfect Moslem wife," she said, nodding to everyone.

"There is too much looking for pleasure these days," said the Frenchwoman, surprising us, rising unsteadily out of her chair. "Everything was
clearer in the past. We knew our roles. We didn't expect to have everything. Well!" she said brightly, turning to Le Mouleau as we all rose to our
feet. "I'll leave you young people to decide about everything. I'm having
dinner tonight with a lady even older than myself, whose husband made the
plans for the trans-Saharan railway. Think of it! Three million five hundred
thousand square miles of desert to cross (incredible that I've remembered),
and it was never built!" With this, she made her way to the door.

After she left, I took off my shoe and swatted a cockroach so large it was almost like killing a stray animal.

"Don't bother, honey," said the woman from television. "You kill one, and all the others come to the funeral."

She laughed, hands on hips, tilting backwards. "We'll turn him into an African yet," she said to Le Mouleau, passing the front desk. "He'll learn to take things *easy*. Come on, you promised to take me swimming." And she slowly sashayed out of the door, her red boubou rustling.

Outside, confidently coming towards us, was the French industrialist I had met at the airport, now unaccompanied by his dog, with a petite Senegalese taking short quick steps behind him to keep up. He passed into the hotel without seeing me, the girl running by in a blur of purple and brown and Arpège.

There are few beaches in Dakar, but one of the luxury hotels has a swimming pool, adjacent to the rocks and the rough Atlantic. A group of American Marines had just arrived, or just landed, immediately setting up a diving competition among themselves. They exhibited their skills, their tattoos; they diligently splashed each other and horsed around and were quite prepared to conquer without effort this hotel pool where most of the swimmers and guests were prepared to simply get out of their way. But from out of nowhere, an African as black as carbon with a superhuman build walked up casually to the diving board. He looked around at the assembled United States Marines in their regulation boxer trunks (he was wearing the smallest of scarlet suits) and then he dove into the pool. It was a swan dive so perfect that the hotel guests gasped; then he swam back to the ladder, repeated the ideal dive and left the pool. The Marines quieted down.

A Frenchwoman lay spread-eagled on her mattress near us, half naked, baking in the sun.

"That woman," said the African with the scarlet suit to my actress friend, "that woman over there would never forget the good time I'd give her."

"She wouldn't forget your dive, if she'd seen it," she said.

"I'm not talking about my dive," he said. Then he giggled.

"Well, what are you talking about?" asked the actress, amused.

"This," he said, pointing to what looked like a subsidiary limb slung in his bathing suit. The giggle broke out into a hearty laugh.

"Haven't you found a place for that yet?" she asked, standing, putting her hands on her hips to study him like a garment on a rack. "You've been carrying that thing around as long as I've known you." Then she went in for a swim.

"We Senegalese are known for it," he said, still studying the Frenchwoman, who dozed unaware.

"You should put it," I said, "in your brochures." Then I stood up to follow my friend into the water.

"Do you know any girls who'd like to correspond with me?" he asked enthusiastically. "I'd send them my picture."

Although several names came to mind, I said that I had enough troubles of my own.

When I left him, I noticed that one of the Frenchwoman's eyes had miraculously opened, but the man in the scarlet bathing suit, unadvised, had walked away.

The sense of timing is a personal characteristic, but it is also part of a larger, national disposition. In Senegal, plans evolve in a lethargic sequence; they ooze, like amoebae across a slide. Tea stretches into and absorbs drinks; then, slowly, drinks pry apart only to reassemble as dinner. Continually I was told that I moved too quickly, that it was not the African Way. The great lassitude there was a strange counterpoint to the most frenetic juxtaposition of images and sounds that has ever come my way. It was impossible to meditate upon one moment, so cluttered was it by coexisting elements. Soon I was to leave. I have always wanted to go away from places, to arrive at the airport holding nothing but a pair of gloves—driving gloves—free of the usual conglomeration that manages to make me such a spectacle. In leaving Dakar, I was attended not only by my array of brimming baggage (the bright cloths of Senegal filling out the last of the vacant spaces), but by a mass of images so vivid that they have remained with me since. I have tried to imprison certain moments here.

Sounds: at the same instant, on a street corner, these layers. *Alouette, gentille Alouette*, sung in childish treble from behind a schoolroom window while a sheep bleats next to a fence, a woman screams in an unknown language to a crying child, and a truck, thundering by, shakes loose one of a pile of watermelons, which lands in the street with a thud as someone who has been trailing along wearing a pair of overalls asks, *"Ça va?"*

And sights: You sit in a café and watch the Frenchwoman—its owner—working on a needlepoint tapestry, a miniature of the Unicorn in the Garden. Flies settle on the sugar bowl at her table; a woman squats, unbuttons her blouse on the sidewalk next to the hedge bordering the café, settling in to sell peanuts to the passersby while nursing her baby. The café owner carefully selects from a basket just the right sylvan shade for the leaf gradually adhering to a finished branch. A man carrying a slatted carton of canaries stops for a moment in front of your table, and shifts his burden; all the crowded canaries lean over on their perch, rustling crazily. Yellow feathers float in the air, the birds, one by one, right themselves, and he and they are gone. You look idly at the traffic, noticing suddenly a dead grey cat at the curb behind the tire of a truck, your view all at once benevolently obscured by a group of passing boys proudly grasping at a tape recorder as they pass it around, each one wanting to possess it if only for a moment, as it blasts *Midnight at the Oasis* into the boulevard, into the hot air now bringing rivulets of perspiration down the neck of the café owner as she bends to finish the leaf of that bosky scene.

From far away the tallest of women comes billowing, lifting along in purples and lilacs. Pierced into and suspended from her ears, large silver hoops brush against her neck; her satin arms are covered in golden bracelets. She is majestic, a priestess of black Africa in her long, flowing gowns with her high cheekbones, her tilted eyes, long lashes and her perfectly carved nose. She approaches the curb, tall—no, the tallest—of all ladies. With an elegant gesture she raises two elongated fingers to her nostrils, stoops ever so slightly and lustily blows her nose into the gutter. The Frenchwoman yawns without disguise, takes off her glasses and rubs her eyes. Then she stares straight ahead, her canvas now forgotten in her lap, the basket of wools now closed. It is almost dusk, and a mosquito, in the first breeze of the day, is heading towards her pale shoulder.

Chapter Five

THE UNITED ARAB EMIRATES: ABU DHABI

There is a land in southern Arabia known as the Empty Quarter. Nothing dwells, nothing grows, nothing moves in daylight. A chill wind sweeps across the vast desert at night changing the pattern of the dunes as a private entertainment. Then the day breaks. The landscape, smooth as velvet and still cool, quickly turns into giant designs of light and shadow, aroused now in the heat, its edges singeing the Persian Gulf. There is no surf. Next to the sand the water is a quiet band of turquoise. The sky is immaculate. The coast becomes three bright ribbons of color, a banner of the elements: earth, water and air wavering under the force of the implied fourth, the fire.

Along the coast, lean, grave bedouins searched for scraps of pasturing land. A gazelle was sighted. It was a miracle, a sign that the place could sustain life. The chieftain decided to settle in, naming the land Abu Dhabi, the Father of the Gazelle. The geographers of the time knew nothing about this. Thirteen colonies had just broken away from England. The Father of the Gazelle, set out against the flawless banner of the elements, was no more than a vagrant shell singing into the ear of no one.

Eventually the British took notice, wishing to provide themselves a safe passage through the Persian Gulf untroubled by the natives. By now there were sheiks ruling small impoverished villages. The British did not choose to colonize. Nothing was there but specks and parings. They decided, instead, to *protect*. Their political agents staggered off boats into the mighty heat, their skins shriveling. They were accommodated. They attempted to put things in order, adjusting themselves with difficulty to diets of dried fish, dates and camel's milk. Later on it would be said that by protecting rather than colonizing they let the natives preserve their traditional sociopolitical organizations. But it was still the nineteenth century and the terminology was more poetical. With a series of treaties and truces haggled over and eventually agreed upon by those grave tribal bedouins and the sweltering British, the land became known as the Trucial Coast. Then it was placed formally on the map; that word *Trucial* was peculiar but it stuck in the mind.

Beneath the changing patterns of the dunes where almost nothing dwelled lurked another miracle, a serious miracle, intact for a million years. It needed only to be found. The local sheiks granted concessions for drilling, offering percentages to entice the foreigners. It sounded as though it was at the end of the world, and it was. Engineers arrived in tiny planes, landing on the hard-packed sand near the sheik's small fortress. In tatters, local Arabs peered over the strangers' shoulders. Drilling equipment was hauled off boats anchored in the harbor. The primeval setting along the coastline was now confused with metal rigs and men with helmets barking orders. The oil did not spurt up as it does in the movies, with everyone standing back, covered (in postures of astonishment) with shiny black. Oil was coaxed from beneath the seabed. Then it was discovered deep below the sand. Each of the Trucial States searched for it with a frenzy, piercing the sands and seabeds. Oil was found and found again. The Trucial Coast, soon to become the United Arab Emirates, went wild. And the Father of the Gazelle stared obliquely at the turquoise sea, never to be the same again.

"Loved the party. Bye-bye darling, see you tomorrow for tea," someone says. Then, with light steps, she patters across a pavement; a car door closes with a heavy, effective click—it is a substantial car—and the hot desert air is temporarily disturbed as the automobile accelerates luxuriously along the Cornish, the municipality's Anglicized interpretation of *corniche*, the six lane boulevard now fronting the Persian Gulf in Abu Dhabi.

"Welcome," says the Japanese hostess after watching the car drive away. "Much going. Much coming. Welcome to, ah, Space City." And with that she titters, extending her small, sallow hand.

Among the foreigners, everyone has come running, sniffing out the prosperity. The atmosphere is that of an overheated, flattened Magic Mountain. Their shared ailments have all—or almost all—centered around money. When these disorders are corrected (and everyone leaves, hopefully, with riches) there will be little sentiment about the place. Behind them, the foreigners will have left polyestrene and plumbing factories, desalinization projects and milk pasteurization plants. They will have introduced Kentucky Fried Chicken stands and private clubs (British), and they will have rented condominiums for fifty thousand dollars a year. They will return home to cities— real cities—with tree lined boulevards and opening nights. Only occasionally will they recall with nostalgic pleasure the nightly program featuring the Ruler of Abu Dhabi himself, a box of tissues inexplicably on display in the foreground, appearing on his own national Abu Dhabi television.

Everywhere there are consultations, there are deals, there are connections

being made. At the pool of the hotel you can see businessmen making tabulations on pocket computers while cautiously taking the sun. Phones ring in the poolside cabanas and it is London or Geneva on the line. Even with the cabana doors closed you can hear heavily accented voices gleefully naming figures that sound like population estimates rather than dollars. You can meet a man who might have just sold the government a shipload of portable latrines as he emerges dripping from the pool. You can see yourself reflected in the mirror lenses of a man in the construction business from Beirut who is worth, they say, five million dollars. On his plump chest, resting on the curled grey and black hairs, are several massive chains of gold. One of them supports the charm against the Evil Eye, another is worked with small jewels spelling "ALLAH" in Arabic. Is there a tiny cross as well? But he moves away. Stewardesses pose on mattresses in attitudes of nonchalance, pretending not to be on the alert for a really big fish to get them off those planes. Boys from Pakistan and India hurry by with trays of drinks, and the Muzak, all-powerful, all-knowing, blares out *Blue Heaven*.

There is a sudden shriek at the side of the pool. Tearing her hair in the passionate and wholly unself-conscious way of primitive Arab women in distress—comportment neither expected nor encouraged at the Hilton—a figure comes rushing forth, a small child in her arms opening its mouth to cry. Everyone stops, horrified, watching her run. Then, with dawning comprehension, they turn back to the pool, where a man is being dragged up, gurgling for breath, his face ashen. Someone near him pounds his back. Someone else runs to the phone. His color darkens. The stewardessess drop their little beach bags. The Pakistani and Indian waiters are frozen into stone, their trays still balanced. The phones keep ringing from London, from Geneva. Several bathers surround the man, turning him this way and that. The shrieking woman can be heard in the hallways. *Blue heaven and you and I* nags in the air, and the man, now purple, heaves up in one, final, primeval motion, and a puddle of pool water emerges from his mouth. A breath follows. Again he brings up pool water. His skin has paled. His head is on the turquoise tiles. He lifts his hand up in a kind of wave, a gesture of reassurance. The immobilized poolside crowd is released into their representational poses. The waiters, again in motion, thread their way past the chairs. The wife is brought back from the hallways, her child now crying in bewilderment and terror. The woman's hair is like a fright wig, with long black strands clutching at her neck. The man is brought staggering to a mattress, waving away offers of assistance. His gold necklace glints in the sunlight; his jeweled Allah, and his charms twinkling as he puts his head down on the pillow.

"Five million bucks," whispers someone with a British accent trying to give it an American twist. "You'd think the bloody bastard could afford swimming lessons."

All of them had thought of his money, ebbing away with his life in a cupful of chlorinated pool water. There is no escape from this constant referral to money. It is the basis on which everything in the sheikdom revolves: it, and its creator, the oil. It has made all things possible, things never imagined even by the greatest Arab fabulists. Abu Dhabi, with its native population of forty thousand—and its invasion of four hundred thousand who have come to participate in the riches it promises—is the richest country in the world.

One tries to forget the designation *the richest country* (in Dubai, up the coast, as we shall see, resides someone billed as *the richest man*). In any case, the implication of opulence is immediately forgotten when one walks through the town of Abu Dhabi, which is roughly the size of Manhattan reshaped into a triangle. The town of Abu Dhabi, incidentally, is in the country of Abu Dhabi—which is not a proper country but a sheikdom incorporated into a Federation of Seven Emirates—but let it pass. So in Abu Dhabi town, dazed by the heat, blinded by the sun, one gropes one's way across half-built sidewalks suddenly ending in rubble and sand and open drains. One keeps watching one's feet, like a goat, to get a grip on the solid parts. The sound of drilling and jackhammering, of welding and cement mixing fuse with the radio and cassette players tinnily hawking Arab dirges, Indian ragas and the latest Salsa rock music; even *Tits and Ass*, from an American musical, finds its way to the local radio station, bleating indecipherably into the air as women, not only veiled but masked underneath by something resembling pickerel skulls sheathed in black, bundle by.

The aural chaos precisely imitates the hugger-mugger of the visual. Air conditioners are omnipotent. They drip on one's head from the stories above; they blow at one's groin from the low shops below. Hoists and pulleys drag them up into the air to fill the square holes punctured for them. The buildings loom on all sides of the arrow-straight boulevards. They are architectural anomalies, architectural anonymities, hustled together on land worth (money again) hundreds of dollars a square foot—more, it is said, than on that similar-sized island of Manhattan and the price is rising.

The traffic snarls. Sheiks, or what pass as sheiks, sit white-robed at the wheels of custom-built Buicks, their sunglasses glinting maliciously, anxious to get those cars in motion. One hops, one skips, one lurches inelegantly out of the way, just missing a truck coming from the other direction carrying forty Pakistanis like a a herd of cattle to a building site where the earlier shift is about to have a collective sunstroke. Here, there is a sudden section of shops newly opened, running with many impediments down a side street. Cars have parked on unfinished sidewalks where merchandise is being uncrated and carried into shops called Playboy, called Jean's Jeans, called Wow! The potential customers cannot study the window displays, so busy are they avoiding the potholes, the craters, the crates and the parked cars in their endeavor to stay whole. There are no dogs and cats; there are no leaners and loafers. Everyone has something to do, everyone is kept nimble. No one beckons, no one asks, *Ça va?*, no one has a hand out. There are no stalls, no folks weave or dye or hammer metal, no one squeezes juices or holds a monkey and no one shines shoes. But there are banks, and there are banks; banks being built and banks enlarging. Banks are more common than bread shops.

The place cries out for a history. Where there is poverty, no one much cares to discover which cave went back to when, which urn applies to what era. But wealth brings with it an interest in antecedents.

"You must begin," said an adviser to the Ruler of Abu Dhabi, "by seeing the relics of our past."

I was seated in his office. Someone was serving me a small glass of cardamom-flavored coffee. Everyone was cordial. Bad manners have yet to be imported. I sat back among the cushions.

His telephone rang. When he concluded his conversation, his telephone

rang again. We could not manage more than brief sentences between calls.

"Someone is coming to Abu Dhabi from the Washington *Post*," he said confidentially, cupping his hand over the receiver. "They are coming from all over. We are like"—he considered it—"a new best seller."

The office was well worn. There were coffee stains on the shag carpet. The sheikdom was apparently frugal in furnishing its bureaucratic offices: a good sign. The door was open and a constant stream of ministry employees came and went with handfuls of paper. Someone sitting next to me was listening with ambition to all conversations at once. He had been appointed—

and later dismissed—as my guide. But his mind, understandably, was on more important matters. He observed the inflowing and outflowing of robed officials.

"He's the Head Minister," he said, thinking I ought to know.

"He's in charge of the Press," he said, less awed.

"He's your driver," he said, passing over it to listen to another conversation. I stared at the carpet and tried to consume the coffee. Again talking on the phone, the adviser motioned to me that he would only be a minute longer. He was a Palestinian. Successful young Arabs in the Middle East are frequently from Palestine, exiled, this generation's Wandering Jews, brilliantly making themselves indispensable to the communities in which they have settled. It took a miscalculation on the part of a foreigner, Balfour, to scatter a million of them as refugees throughout the world.

"Tonight," said the adviser, "I must go to London." He smiled. "And not just for my wardrobe. Business! Affairs of State!"

He tapped the side of his head with a pencil. "You come highly recommended. You will be the guest of the state. I suggest that you begin by visiting the museum at Al Ain. Our history, you see . . ."

I had not expected a museum.

And so it was that I found myself, still staggering from the delirium of Space City, about to set off to explore its past.

"My assistant will arrange it all. And when I come back from London we'll dine." And then, uncharacteristically for a Moslem, he added, "You must meet my wife."

I was ushered out. He was again on the phone. I was going one hundred and sixty kilometers into the desert to see a museum. He was flying thirty five hundred miles to London. In the past, Englishmen craved the vast spaces of Araby. Now the Arabs are magnetized by Fortnum and Mason's.

In an outer office, a typist transcribed my virtues into Arabic and a document was handed to me, full, I imagined, of eloquent praise. I still have it somewhere. On its crest a gold eagle supports in its breast a kind of porthole which, against a crimson sky, lies a schooner.

As I waited for my itinerary the coffee server stood next to me poised to pour another glass. I had not been able to lose him.

"You must shake your glass from side to side to signify that you've had enough," said someone taking pity, "or they will pour into eternity."

I did this, accomplishing a kind of magic, for he disappeared in a flash.

The adviser was still talking on the phone when I finally left.

The dual highway cuts straight through the desert without a curve. You do not bother about the heat. The driver has the air-conditioning indicator up to *coldest*. It is useless to complain that it is too cold. If you open the window a crack the enveloping hot air issues from the outside world faster than it would from a pierced tire. The driver looks back over his shoulder at you, rolling his eyes, and you quickly close it. The music on his cassette is of a Greek singing in heavily accented English. "Stronjahs een di noit . . ." If you shut your eyes, you are in an air-conditioned nightclub at three in the morning instead of spinning across the Arabian desert at high noon inside a space capsule launched from Space City. The sky is white hot. The billboards you pass advertise large glasses of milk: MILKA milk. Others, their messages in Arabic and in English, say, "Be Cool!" Painted with colors fast fading in the sun, air conditioners fly through imagined Alpine air, with snowcapped Swiss mountains in the shape of pyramids.

Down the middle of the highway there is a line of the frailest of saplings propped up against sticks. Oleanders and eucalyptus and various feathery palms seem like mythical supplicants under the fiery sun. Anything that grows is penned in; then it is tended like a foundling. Immense water trucks ply the highway day and night, and ministering angels in the form of Baluchis and Pakistanis hop out at intervals, wearing patterned dhotis. The absence of color in this dry landscape is so total that these sudden scraps of cloth and the colored, translucent hose are startling. Water floods out—water as precious here as oil is elsewhere—and the small trees and bushes are almost submerged. The assistant waterer looks on, his soaked dhoti tucked up to his waist, his turban askew. Now they are joined by a third man, the driver, wearing a khaki uniform. With hands behind his back he watches over the watering, something skeptical in his posture. He investigates the plant and removes a dead leaf. The three of them surround the row of plantings that sag in the heat, the desert stretching out on all sides of them to the horizon. The sand swallows up the water in one gulp, patted dry in an instant by the insatiable sun.

The driver stops the car to pray. He walks a few steps away from the highway. He bobs up; then he disappears as though seeking something. Then he is up, then he is down. You are left inside the car with the Greek still singing. An occasional car or truck passes at great speed, rocking you in its wake, and calmly, after symbolically washing his hands following the prayers, the driver slowly walks over to the car to re-enter the century.

The silence sensed outside the automobile is complete. Not even flies buzz here. The dunes begin to grow in size. From the flat edges of the desert they march across the horizon. Soon they are giant toast-colored waves hundreds of feet high. The landscape is, all at once, remarkable, larger than life; the dunes are out of a legend. Then just as quickly they vanish. They were reminders, only, of the great desert in the Empty Quarter. Now the town of Al Ain is just ahead. It is built mainly of mud. Someone has said that it could be destroyed with a water pistol.

In front of the museum there were several police cars and big, flashy motorcycles. Uniformed guards gathered around its entrance, and my creden-

tials were checked (but not read) by someone with hennaed fingernails. An unnaturally secure building, it seemed, pressed against a mud fortress on the edge of an oasis. Inside the lobby the Palestinian woman who ran the galleries was summoned. I was surprised to see a woman. In neighboring Saudi Arabia women are not even allowed to drive cars; stones and rocks are thrown at them for adultery; they stay indoors. She stared at me nervously. Then she disappeared into her office; there were whispered consultations. I looked around, glancing into one of the guarded galleries. The atmosphere was of a public school exhibition inside Fort Knox.

"I will show you around," said the woman just before I wandered into one of the rooms, and she walked briskly ahead of me towards the glass cases.

"We don't have the relief of the man riding the camel—perhaps the first such find—dating from 2700 B.C. As I say, we don't have it. But it comes from this area. We were a main trade route to the East, you know. You see, the pottery here"—she gestured vaguely towards the case—"is similar to that found in southern Baluchistan, quite far away."

I looked into the glass case, watching the reflection of the woman looking nervously over her shoulder.

I said, "If this is a bad moment for me to have come . . ."

"No. No, not at all." She went on to the next case to continue her speech.

"Circumcision tools," she said. Then she sneezed.

There was a rustle behind us and two men came in, walked to a display counter and pretended to study the copper route to Mesopotamia.

"Detectives," she said in spite of herself.

"This place seems unusually well guarded," I said. "I'm sure you have some valuable things, of course."

"Well, you see"—she glanced quickly at her watch—"within five minutes we are going to be visited by a prince from Saudi Arabia and his entourage."

"And he wants the place to himself."

"They are always fearful."

"But why didn't you tell me?"

"You, too, are a guest of the state," she said timidly. "Our scheduling got mixed."

"But, after all, a *prince* . . ."

She turned away to smile.

I maneuvered my way to a rear building just as the motorcade drew up to the entrance. Sirens split the noon quiet. The escorts gunned their motors like Hell's Angels, and then the only sound was of footsteps and the swish of long robes accompanied by bootheels clicking to attention.

I watched, of course, from a space near the wall. Everyone had suddenly converged; everything electrified. Bright lights, television cameras appeared out of nowhere. Falcons were produced to perch obligingly on the gloves of men strategically placed within the cameras' range—the Sheik of Abu Dhabi is a zealous falconer—and the prince swirled in his robes to the museum's doors. Briefly he hovered there, his entourage assembling nearby. They all seemed to be treading water. Then in an instant it was all over. The lights were out, the cameras were gone, the falcons had disappeared. Only the guards were left outside, lighting cigarettes.

I was escorted to the oasis at Al Ain by a taciturn man shaped like a goldfish; that is, he lacked some articulation between his sloping shoulders and his head, so that whenever he spoke, his entire stocky form turned to me in the back seat of the car. When I asked him where he was born, he took a while before answering. *Bethlehem*, he said gravely, making it sound like a reproach. I told him that it certainly sounded like a fine place to be born, he grunted, and we barely spoke again.

"History? *Forget* it!" said a German woman in what she considered the latest American slang. She happened past me as I emerged from the car at the oasis. I must have been trying to unearth some information from the Bethlehem gentleman and she had overheard my questions. She was a thin middle-aged woman with yellow hair who worked in the one carpet store in

Abu Dhabi and she wore blue denim studded with nail heads.

"Everything in the Emirates is NOW! No past!" she continued, flailing her arms about in some inexplicable semaphore. Clearly she was an animated woman.

I thanked her distractedly for the information, drowsy in the heat. Energetic people in hot places increase my fatigue. The insects hummed; orange wasps hovered over the sluggish water in the felajs—the ancient irrigation canals—and the palm fronds lazily clacked against each other. I considered lying next to the canal and drifting off to sleep.

"I've seen you with your friends in Abu Dhabi," she persisted. "I'm giving a party. For Halloween. I've been to New York. To Bloomingdales. Everyone will be there. You must come."

"Halloween?" my voice cracked.

"But don't bring that Syrian friend of yours," she added unwisely, referring, I recalled in retrospect, to a Sunni from Aleppo. "A Jew, if ever I saw one." She pronounced the word *chew*. "I know." She said, tapping the side of her nose. "I can sniff them out." She smiled.

My eyes narrowed down. Quickly she added, "It will be a good party." She tilted her head in the direction of my Yemenite driver. "There will be only white faces."

It was breathtaking that she managed to give voice in such quick succession to the two time-worn prejudices no local person I encountered in the Moslem world had ever ventilated.

"Madam," I said, "M-madam," stammering, never finding the right words when my adrenalin drowns them. "You are the debris of the western world." Then I walked away, wide awake, with a headache, leaving her, I'm sure, none the wiser, thinking that she had encountered some kind of stuttering loon, and no doubt relieved that I avoided her party.

The history of this coast is sparse. Communal graves have been found dating back two and three thousand years. Some of them are decorated with tracings of bulls and oryx, and there is that camel relief, a find of some significance, the earliest evidence of the animal being ridden by man, the first known ship of the desert. There are copper fishhooks and limestone weights, and it seems that a trading post existed connecting this coast with Mesopotamia, Persia, and the Indus. Then it must have died—as civilizations have frequently died—when other trade routes were discovered, leaving no monuments to its memory.

Now the freighters lie at anchor for weeks, even for months, waiting to deposit the things a rich country demands, to deliver the massive orders. Everything in Abu Dhabi comes from somewhere else except for the fish, a few small crops, and the oil. Even the oil has to be sent elsewhere to be refined. By the time it returns it is expensive. You cannot drive up to a gasoline station and fill up a tank for a dollar. The sand, too, is the wrong sand for use in construction. The grains are round rather than sharp, and they do not adhere. The final indignity is that sand has to be imported.

The freighters are kept so long at anchor way out in the harbor, massed there for months, that crews have been known to mutiny. The merchandise, too, reacts to the delays. There is the persistent story of the rice. Too long was it kept at anchor, in the hold, under the boiling sun, too long did it absorb the atmosphere. It began to swell. And it cooked. Way out on the horizon it pushed its way through the hatches and the portholes, heaping high on the decks, the astonished sailors leaping out of its way. At night, the long

chain of boats with their lights stretching as far as the eye can see is referred to as the Golden Necklace.

The bazaar, newly designed, is not a bazaar, it is a compartmentalized supermarket. Gone are the heavy shadows associated with the souqs, the deep vaults of commerce. The sounds, too, are missing: no tintinnabulations from the brass market, no soft shuttles click against the looms. Nothing tempts, nothing lures; you pass through the neat streets of the bazaar unwooed. All the doors are shut. The stalls inside are air-conditioned to the gills. Once in-

side these cool cubicles no one plies you with mint tea or thick coffee. The shopkeepers arrange and rearrange their standardized stock, muttering to themselves in the dialects of their long lost homes. Even the local Arab merchants, now cool, now comfortable, are as indifferent as salespeople along the Faubourg St. Honoré. You buy, or you don't buy, and that's that.

At the hour of the muezzin's chant, you can see, in the shop windows of the appliance stores, a dozen television screens tuned to the local station. The studio muezzin recites to the assembled window shoppers duodecimally, surrounded by digital computers and stereo sets. Late at night, you can again hear the muezzin across the darkened condominium rooftops, filling the night air with the fierce power of Islam generating from the sacred black stone, the Ka'ba of Mecca, far across the Empty Quarter. A phrase is repeated and repeated again; a grating sound of static hangs over Abu Dhabi. Then there is an instant of complete silence. A needle is picked up from some great groove in the sky and the chant is resumed further down on the record. The same recording is being played in Damascus, in Baghdad, in Alexandria. The tall minarets piercing the sky are all plugged into the nineteen seventies.

Quickly, the Seven Emirates are the following: Abu Dhabi, Dubai, Sharjah, Ras al Khaimah, Umm al Qaiwain, Ajman and Fujairah. They are also known as sheikdoms. The first three have discovered oil. There is a possibility that oil exists in Ras al Khaimah, but the last three emirates hold little hope for this miracle. There is an unrelieved desert between each of these cities. Periodically, spaced about one kilometer apart along the highway, automobile wrecks have been placed on weathering platforms to discourage accidents, to remind drivers, as it says on signs along the way, *We do not want to lose you.* These skeletal cars become a kind of sculpture exhibition set out along the sand.

I was being driven to Dubai. The driver, Mohammed, was from Abu Dhabi.

"I will marry an Indian girl," he said, turning down the radio.

I asked what she was like.

"I haven't met her yet. My uncle married an Indian girl. They're pretty. They don't ask for much of a dowry. A hundred dollars. Here, it's four thousand plus another fifteen hundred for the wedding. Too much for an Abu Dhabi girl."

"Maybe you could find one who's . . . less expensive."

Mohammed ignored the possibility. "I want twelve children," he said. "The government gives me fifty dollars a month for each child. That's . . ."

We tried to work it out. Another crashed Fiat passed on its platform. I was accustomed, now, to hearing about money all the time.

"Six hundred dollars," I said. It was beginning to be economically in-

teresting. "You get six hundred dollars a month for a dozen children."

"Also, the children are paid money to stay in school and learn. Also, we get some food from the government, and there is a contribution to the house. Hospitals, too, are paid for. Also, when the babies come, hospitals are very correct. The wives put on their masks and veils as soon as the babies are born. They don't lie there with their faces out."

I thought about that.

"My wife would only see my mother and a few friends."

"What about the heat? She might not be accustomed, if she's from India."

"Air conditioning. Everything is filled with it."

"And if she wants to work?" I thought I'd run the gamut.

Mohammed looked mystified.

"A job," I said.

"A *job?*" he said. "*Aib!*" It is a word frequently heard. It means "shame."

Then, after a pause, he asked, "How much does a wife cost in New York?"

I thought awhile before answering. The sand stretched to all horizons.

"Nothing."

"What do you mean, nothing?"

"Nothing," I repeated. "They're free."

He puzzled over that for almost a kilometer.

"*Aib,*" he said finally. "Their families shouldn't just *give* them away. They should take some profit."

Chapter Six

TO DUBAI AND BACK

Dubai seems a city of displaced persons. They group in the streets, quickly made friends from similar places longing to be elsewhere. They go everywhere in truckfuls. They do everything in company. They are without their families; the language is not theirs, nor are the clothes, nor are the habits, nor is the land. They stare as much at someone in local dress, called here dishdasha, as they do at foreigners wearing what appears to be bulletproof polyester, for they themselves, dressed as they were back home, are only here on consignment, passing through, even though the passage might be for years, for generations. There are Indians, gathering around movie posters on their days off, gawking at the promises of SEXY MIRACLE, AN INDIAN FILM, long before the show is ready to begin, trying to stretch the time, trying to enlarge the experience. There are Pakistanis from Karachi, from the Punjab, from Sind, each of them speaking their own language, each of them sealed off from each other, and together sealed off from the Arabs. There are Pathans from Afghanistan with their wide, saucered turbans. From Baluchistan there are tribal men with craggy faces, without a country for twenty years and once again homeless. There are Iranian youths who crossed the borders and the Persian Gulf to avoid the draft, now unable to return. They have all funneled here like the residue next to a drain after a heavy rain. They cannot realize their worth, how essential they are to the building of a contemporary city, because they know how easily they can be replaced. There are always others standing by on those foreign shores, needing the money with the same desperation as they, ready to arrive in crowded planeloads with cardboard suitcases and fresh, blank passports.

They build Dubai during the day and they continue to build it at night. Surrounded by darkness, within the glare of spotlights, they weld, they cement, they drill; the great buildings rise like phantoms under their efforts. The Pyramids were created by men in this way, though they were called

slaves then, corralled together similarly but not paid. These laborers from distant places have brought their poverty with them like a contagion; they cannot rid themselves of it. Most of their paychecks are put into envelopes and sent home along with sentimental notes neatly typed by the scribes who mass near the post offices, each with his typewriter, each with his native language, listening or not bothering to listen to the sad tales they are told. Even when they seem to settle in and give up thoughts of returning home, even when, one by one, their families come to join them, their neighborhoods are cloaked in their poverty, tucked in among the new skyscrapers they themselves are building.

Along with the bright caged parrots shrieking their languages, they have smuggled in sacred cows and elderly relations who live, as they did back home, on begging, thrusting out their infirmities as they must have done in Bombay; promised, I suppose, to be more richly rewarded here for the shock they have inflicted on the unaccustomed passersby. At the brightly lit fruit and vegetable stalls where the moneyed foreigners have learned to shop, the beggars wait, along with the wandering cows, turning it into an area of India. Cars drive up, screech to a halt; the rich, with a Western determination, go right to the merchandise, pick, choose, pay, bend back into their station wagons with their filled bags—for all the world as though they were in Greenwich, Connecticut—and pull away. The cows, undisturbed, their gentle faces unworried, stand in the way, interrupting the wide arcs as the cars reverse to zoom away. Then the cows step aside, slowly, permitting the beggars an extra minute for pleading.

Shifting their feet, the foreign laborers stand in long lines in front of the ministries, their papers, their passports clutched, smudged, smeared. They, too, are required to make their pleas for favors. It is the tradition in the Moslem world. At an intersection, a man's sheaf of papers is blown out of the bus window by an unexpected gust of desert wind. He scrambles out to rush down the road in madness, separated by an unseen hand from this documentation of his existence. He has stood in line for these papers for months. Back home, he has paid good money for them, he has prayed and planned and schemed to meet the construction man from Araby who has rented a hotel room and set up a desk to do the mass hiring. His family have said their goodbyes at the airport with large, silent eyes, with many promises and many doubts. And here he is in the center of a place called Dubai on the edge of a giant-sized Arab world unknown to him, running after these forms, the duplicates, the triplicates heavy with hard-won signatures and stamps that verify his right to be there. Without them he is a vagrant. He is less than he was back home. He snatches a paper felled by an upended carton, he grabs at another sheet, the sun full in his eyes. The paper shimmers, the sun passing through it, and he squints at it and runs on. Other papers skid like autumn leaves in the rubble fronting the big buildings going up all around him. He runs this way and that, stooping to pick and fumble. He holds in triumph what he has collected, forgetting in that instant, before he studies them, that he cannot read and might not know whether they are his.

The big banks breathe heavily over the multitudes, their air conditioners just above the sidewalk level where everyone hurries by. There is a bank for every fourteen hundred residents. No one can escape thinking about money. Rarely does someone move off to be alone; solitude belongs in the lost world of the bedouins. But in the small park near one of the banks, in the last light of the day, next to an oleander in full flower, a Moslem from Baluchistan removes his slippers, faces the lost sun, places his turban, unwound, beneath his knees and prays, his lips moving soundlessly. Then, when he is through, another Moslem occupies that small space next to the oleander. *In the name of Allah, the Compassionate, the Merciful . . .* sanctifying the place with their prayers. The one oleander blooms profusely; the others are overgrown, with no flowers. It is a mystery. It is a benediction. The lights in the park do not go on because there are no bulbs, the fountains are without water and the park benches are made of stone. The mu-

nicipality's money is being spent elsewhere. Contemplation is not encouraged.

The ruling sheik presides over much of the fortune that sweeps into Dubai, alert as a croupier with his rake. The telephone company, the electric company are mainly his; so is the ferry service and the public taxi system. There is also his real estate and his construction; there is the air and sea transport. But enumeration is useless. I had forgotten the oil. Great riches were known here even before the oil. Dubai was the center of gold smuggling from the Arabian Peninsula to the East. In the 1950's, the sheik was the partner of the customs inspector—sent there by the British to supervise the customs operations. The two of them created an empire. Gold was sent to India in motorized dhows across the Persian Gulf. In India there is a preference for gold: Gold means Rich. The customs man and the sheik were only carrying on a tradition established in Dubai since the time of the pirates and still going strong. Gold arrives from the Middle East and England and Switzerland and is smuggled to India and Pakistan and often to Iran.

Now the customs man is Dubai's Minister of Petroleum, he is Dubai's Ambassador to England, to Paris, to Scandanavia. He has amassed an art collection here and a street of Georgian houses there; castles in Britain and mines in Africa are reputed to be his; so are large percentages of most of Dubai's bigger business deals. He is uncertain whether he is, as he is fabled to be, the richest man in the world, with something like five billion dollars. But his advice to the average man is memorable. "If you do not know how to use your money," he has said, "you will be more miserable than a poor man. A poor man has nothing to lose. A wealthy man,"—and here is the nice part—"always has something." I have been told that he is an able man, an intelligent man. Recently he was interviewed by an acquaintance whom he allowed, apparently with great cordiality, only ten minutes. "You must understand," he said, "by spending the time talking to you instead of doing business on the phone, I'm losing about a million dollars."

This is the big-time treasure, the kind seen in Technicolor movies when Ali Baba and his men come upon casks in a cave, shimmering, in some off-camera light, with gold and jewels. When sheiks and sultans of the oil-rich countries spend their fortunes on fleets of Cadillacs and immense hideous palaces, we try not to smile, having understood that these are examples of the bad use of money. In London, where the line between what is considered good and what is considered bad is most carefully drawn, such money is courted; then it is feared. Large impossible flats in Mayfair are rented out to oil sheiks at extravagant rates and then everyone complains that laundry now hangs from the wrought-iron terraces. This is where proud Britons once stood to watch Victoria ride by, warmed by the knowledge that the sun never set on her empire. Now they see the Rolls-Royce pull away from the curb and stop; they watch the rear door open, the man in the flowing white garment and dark glasses gets out, relieves himself in a glistening stream next to the tire and then gets back inside. Wide-eyed, they then see the driver, a liveried British gentleman, fling open his front door, raise his hands to heaven, somewhere high above the matched rooftops along the Crescent, and quit on the spot, slamming the door and rocking the Rolls and the white-robed gentleman inside, his bladder now emptied, leaving him to sit anxiously in the back seat alone, wondering how to move the great shining car parked halfway into the traffic.

The story was told to me by an Englishman, who, like almost everyone else in the packed hotels of Dubai, was in town to make a deal. We were sitting in the lobby of the Intercontinental Hotel early in the day.

"IT SIMPLY WON'T DO!" he cried in conclusion. Then he drained his scotch and ordered another.

"What is it?" I asked. "What bothers you so much about the Arabs?"

"EVERYTHING!" he snapped. "Why ELSE would I be ordering whiskey at ten in the morning?"

He had a soggy look. Considering the weather, his shapeless suit could not have been tweed, but it looked it. He was all shambles and shakes.

"They're so arrogant with their new money! But they can't even fix a broken main in the streets without getting a foreigner over to do it. And the corruption! My company sells chemicals. There's supposed to be a limit to the profit they can make here. So they ask us to double our bill—do you follow me?—*double our bill.* Then we have to take half of what they send us and put it in a secret account for them in Switzerland."

I must have looked at him with the blank stare I cannot control when anyone discusses economics.

"You don't follow me, do you?" he asked. Then he looked beyond me, sighing at my incapacity. I have heard that sigh before.

"They *ask* you to charge them twice as much?" I began lamely.

"Look." He cleared his throat. He was going to enunciate each syllable. "My price is *five* thousand pounds. They want me to charge them *ten* thousand pounds. Do you follow me so far?"

I nodded. I considered ordering a scotch for myself.

"So I charge them *ten* thousand pounds. They send it to me. And I put *five* thousand of those pounds, because it's *theirs*, into a bank account they keep in Switzerland."

"And?"

"And then they can say that the chemicals cost them ten thousand pounds. They have our bill to prove it. So they charge *their* customers a price based on that."

I pondered this. "So," I began, always needing to refer things down to their lowest common denominator, "if I go into a store and buy . . ."

"You'll be paying twice what it's worth," he interrupted, anxious to be elsewhere. "Don't speak to ME about Arabs!"

"Would you prefer to discuss British colonial policies?" I asked, about to get onto firmer ground.

"*We* never urinated in public," he said.

It seemed a reasonably good epitaph and I let it go at that.

There are so many nationalities crisscrossing under the noonday sun of Dubai and the other Emirates that there is bound to be a certain disharmony. A Jordanian stands at the front desk of a hotel; the porter is from Yemen, the doorman is from the Sultanate of Oman. They are watched over by an Iraqi engineer whose wife visits a Lebanese hairdresser. And although this is only the beginning, it is enough to give a general idea of the language and dialect problem. The Arabic that is spoken by the natives of the Emirates is only infrequently heard. Although it is their land, and only they can own it, they are almost lost in the shuffling.

"These bloody Abu Dhabians," said a Sudanese temporarily in charge of finding me a room. "Why do they always wait till the last moment to advise us of a visit by a guest of the state?" I told him that I regretted the inconvenience. "In Khartoum," he began, his eyes glazing over with the wonders of the place he left behind, "we arrange things months in advance. You would have been billeted at the Intercontinental straightaway. There would be no need for all this wibble-wobble all over town. It gives me the pip."

"Do you speak any other language?" I asked, trying to shut him up.

Finally, we located "The Creek, Pension, Jane Tsitsimitse Managing Director and Partner." This is what it said on the card. It was located on the upper floor of a new apartment building in a neighborhood still under construction. The workmen from the building opposite had thrown out the excess orange wall-to-wall carpeting, the spreading-flower-design material left over from the upholstery, and the empty crates and cans, and spilled thises and unused thats, where they collected along with the multinational ordures —nobody seems to use the public toilets—in a fading, festering heap.

But back to Mme. Tsitsimitse. She bustled to the front desk. I had gotten unused to bustling. I had grown accustomed to motions which were lazy, and which, when they were not lazy, were uneconomical. She welcomed me. She offered to prepare me a lunch of smoked trout and a salad. I was amazed. The Sudanese accompanying me stepped into the elevator, bent under the weight of the unknown errands and annoyances awaiting him, and disappeared.

"I am Egyptian," announced Mme. T. when I asked her. I had thought, despite the intriguing name, that she was Viennese. Her ample silhouette, her shrewdness and her sudden generosity recalled someone presiding over the pastries in Demels or the Sacher.

"Now the Arabs go to Cairo for what you Americans call Rest and Relaxation. The women in Cairo," she said, with obvious pride, "are rather beautiful. And quite liberated."

"You decided not to stay," I said, edging her towards her story. We were having tea near her pension.

"I *was thrown out*, my dear. After Farouk. The most interesting people were asked to leave. And so I moved. And moved again. It became a habit. So much moving, so many hotels. I decided to go into the hotel business—which I knew nothing about. So I wrote to a long list of hotels in the Middle East."

"And you came to Dubai."

"Dubai? Dubai?" she said, mocking an earlier innocence. "It was the *one* place that answered me and offered me a job. Where *was* Dubai? I couldn't find it on a map! I thought I had invented it. When I wrote back it was like sending a letter into space. They sent me a ticket! *A one-way ticket to Dubai.* Finally, I decided that I didn't want to know where it was. I would *pack*"—she swirled her spoon in the air—"and I would *go*. So just like that I came here. When I got off the plane, it was nighttime. No one was here to meet me. It was like stepping into an oven! In Egypt it was never as hot as this. And so small! Ten years ago, this was. I couldn't even find a taxi. I went to the fence and looked back at the plane: my God! But I couldn't afford to think I'd made a mistake. Then I found a driver willing to take me to the hotel. It was empty! Empty! Not one guest! Someone was sleeping all curled up in the lobby. So, half asleep, he came to the door and said, take a room, take any of the rooms. The owner will be back in a few days. I opened the door of a room. I looked inside. The mattresses were rolled up. I put one of them down—it wasn't a bad mattress—pushed my suitcases against the door and fell asleep like a baby."

"And that's how you came to Dubai."

"That's how everybody came, everybody who didn't just come to do business. For seven years I stayed at that hotel. Then I decided to open a hotel of my own." Her eyes squinted down. "There's a lot of money to be made here. You should get into a business. You're a young man. You could make a fortune. All you need," she said confidentially, "is a local Arab partner. You've got to have one. And don't expect not to be robbed blind." Then she laughed. "But you can still make a fortune."

When tea was over, she consulted my check, narrowing her eyes to locate the total upside down.

"They charge too much in this place," she said. "Now if *I* were to open a restaurant . . ."

Along the quays, there are dhows, moored there like houseboats. On board, solemn Indian boatmen sip tea under torn awnings, gathered around cooking fires. These boats have achieved an aged, respectable shade of grey, recalling, like the feluccas along the Nile, images of ancient times in Arabia. Just next to them there is a row of mirror-bright red motorcycles, with kids all over the place aching to try them out. Probably they are contraband, brought in on those same elderly dhows. A man in charge gives one of the boys instructions. He starts up the motorcycle, it wobbles off along the quay—wobbles, jerks, dies. Other kids run after it and the rider starts it again, trying frantically to make it move before they catch up with him as he now sets out towards Dubai's Cornish, where the traffic glints dangerously: glints and beckons (ah, but the motorcycle man is calling him back). And at dusk, you can imagine, out in the middle of the estuary—The Creek—looking towards the shore now dotted with lights, what Dubai might have been like had they thought to make it beautiful.

SMILE, says the sign as you approach the adjoining Emirate just up the coast, SMILE—YOU ARE IN SHARJAH. You do smile, obeying the prompting, though the smile is for the sign, not for the place. So new is Sharjah, so oil-rich new, and the chaos of building is so complete, that it could be, in the confusion, the opposite: it could be a massive demolition. At first there is no indication that it is a city rising. Field after field of the paraphernalia of a city surrounds you, empty of all life save those crews engaged in putting it together—or pulling it apart. Your eye roams the debris looking for some signs of indigenous activity to humanize it. You understand that only three years ago was oil discovered here, that its territory is exactly a thousand square miles, that the city you see before you grows ten times in volume each year. A small notice atop a two-story building wedged in between scaffolding tells you that it is the Sharjah Hotel and Meat Shop. You stumble upon it as an artifact of the past. Ferreting around, you have found a pre-oil building. So brainwashed have you been by progress, by the absence of a past, you have successfully forgotten the polychrome glazes doming the great mosques of Islam, the tiles and frescoes, the carved wood, the unifying surfaces that have sculptured entire villages, and the ancient Moslem conception that houses are sanctuaries meant to look inward on green, cool places, on fountains. Here you have come upon the Sharjah Hotel and Meat Shop like Schliemann discovering Troy.

It is only when you continue along the desolate sand-swept highway linking all of the Emirates that you realize the absence of prosperity. If you think of the Federation of Seven Emirates as a family—and it is very like one politically, with the same laws, the same currency, the same flag and the same national anthem—then these are the poor relations. You can tell which Emirate you are in not only by the photograph of its Ruler in the shops, but by the volume of its possessions. In Umm al Qaiwain, in Ajman, the traffic has thinned out, the buildings are low, there is lethargy along with the rubble and the flies. Children wearing no shoes poke at things absently; rats scuttle along the shore; nets are being mended with effort; the bay, reflecting the town, is sluggish.

Gone is the razzle-dazzle, gone are the telexes from Geneva, the visitors from the Washington *Post*, the Miró lithographs. The small public park is chained shut. Streetlamps supporting clusters of broken globes are rusting. The dried-out rubber hoses coiled like dead snakes no longer await the water trucks; there are traces of a pattern where flowers were meant to grow spelling out the word "welcome." Remnants of the boom elsewhere have altered everything, so that shreds of neighboring prosperity sift through. A housing development has been contributed, a movie theater; a few foreigners have come, for reasons of their own, hoping, probably, to be there

right at the start, if the oil is ever discovered. There are many small, impossible arguments over honor; there are litigations with the neighboring Emirates—where there is wealth—over certain date trees and grazing fields. It passes the time, it releases the resentment. But it does not lighten the injustice. Everyone waits. Merchants with small shops sit gloomily behind their stalls staring at the trickle of cars passing through, wondering whether the oil has really stopped at the borders.

I stayed in an apartment during my last few days in Dubai. On the day I was to leave I put some coffee on the stove and went downstairs to throw out the garbage, two relatively harmless domestic occupations. Then I realized that I had forgotten my key. Imagining the water gradually boiling away, it was with some urgency that I knocked on the door of the concierge. There was the sound of a nest being disturbed, a kind of rustling, and then a restless re-rustling. "*Meem ala el bab?*" Who is on the door?, came a woman's muffled voice, as though a mouse had lifted the top of a carton.

"I've locked myself out," I said in a stage whisper. "I thought your husband might have a key."

There was a silence, then a scraping.

"I'm staying upstairs," I said, loudly now, trying to sound reliable. "I went downstairs with the garbage and locked myself out."

The scraping gave way to a complicated bolt and key sound. Then a chain was affixed to the other side of the door and it was opened a crack.

"No one is here," said the voice. I could barely distinguish a nose. A hand covered the mouth.

"The keys. The keys," I said. "I only want the keys." In my mind I saw the last of the coffee boil over, I saw the pot growing red hot.

The bolt and key sound in reverse followed the closing of the door.

The hallway was hot; outside it was even hotter. There was the small sound of a motor which grew louder as a motorcycle turned the corner into the rubble-filled back lot of the building and stopped in front of the down-stairs doorway. The concierge lifted himself off the seat with surprising agil-ity considering his bulky shape. Then he clumped inside, stamped the dust and sand off his shoes, eyed me suspiciously and proceeded to unlock his door.

"I locked myself out of my apartment," I said, seizing an appropriate mo-ment when he was inserting a third key in the third of his locks.

"You've locked yourself out?" he repeated. A final meshing of tumblers permitted him to open his door. "Wait!" He held me off with a gesture of his uplifted hand. I stood back obediently. His wife was somewhere behind the door. They whispered to each other. I heard the mouse sounds skitter-ing away. The door was then shut; I could hear another door close; then the front door opened and he beckoned to me.

"Now, enter," he said.

I began my garbage story, irritated at myself for explaining my predica-ment.

"You were taking out the garbage? *Aib!* That is for women to do."

"Well," I said, trying to maintain a good humor, "we're not all perfect."

He was not amused. He repeated the part about the garbage to his wife, who was hiding behind the bathroom door. She tittered in a muffled way. Then, with great trouble, he removed from some high place in a closet a large plastic bag of keys, mumbling to himself as he slowly read the labels at-tached to each of them.

Trying to hurry him, I said, "I . . . left something on the stove." It hurt me to say it.

"You left something on the stove? You COOK? You carry out the GAR-BAGE?"

I heard strange clattering sounds from the bathroom as he transmitted this information to his wife: mirthful clattering sounds.

"Just give me the keys," I said, "and give them to me fast."

"Okay, okay," he said, "but that is not men's work, kitchen work."

Had I been a proper Arab I would have let the house burn down, justify-ing myself, *whitening my face*, as they say. This saving of the face, *wajh*, is the base on which the entire Islamic world displays itself. I thought of this when I had found the key, let myself into the apartment and stood in the kitchen drinking my coffee—the pale jets of gas on the stove bore little connection to the oil boom and the coffee was barely boiling. *Wajh*, like so many words in Arabic, encompasses many concepts: pre-eminence, payment, personal satisfaction, wages, respect. Every detail of behavior has been prescribed. I had briefly forgotten, staying in that condominium with its wall-to-wall carpeting, its abstract lithographs and chromium furniture, that here, ten years ago, there were tents; and here, now, the barbarian was me.

But what remains of the mystery of Arabia, the crossing of its deserts, its solitude?

> *Wend now thy way with brow serene, fear not thy humble tale*
>   *to tell:–*
> *The whispers of the Desert wind; the tinkling of the camel's*
>   *bell.**

The romantic's dream was woven from that. Now the cars swerve around corners, head out along the wide boulevards. At night they pull over to the side of the road, four or five glistening automobiles in the light of street-lamps, parked the way camels must have been before. White-robed gentlemen lean against metal hoods, assembled there to pass the time, telling tales, or secrets, or giving the daily quotations on the gold market.

Even among the foreigners there are one or two who might have come to this place, still lured by earlier promises of adventure. I remembered one of them on my drive back to Abu Dhabi. He was with the foreign service, a young man proud of his accomplishments who wished to convey a sense of timidity. This shyness gave him a particular grace, and it effectively deactivated the more obvious ambition that seemed to characterize everyone else who had come here. He had been living in Jordan, where he taught English, and he took frequent trips out into the desert. There he acquired a bedouin friend and a camel—a blood relative, in fact, to Lawrence of Arabia's camels—and he and the bedouin set out to cross the desert into Saudi Arabia. The rhythm was slow, surprising him: he would see a mountain in the distance and expect to cross it—as he would in a car—in a half hour. But it would take all day, and the days went by slowly. Eventually they reached the enclave of a Saudi sheik who entertained them for a number of days. When it was time for them to leave, the sheik urged them not to continue by camel, fearing the heat and the lack of water. Instead, he packed them off in a truck, along with their camels, and they arrived in Qatar, along the Persian Gulf.

* Sir Richard Burton, *The Kasidah of Haji Abdul el Yezdi* (New York: Alfred A. Knopf, 1924).

Their arrival had been expected. A cable had been received. The local sheik sent a large car to bring them to his fortress, and he gave a party in their honor and took rooms for them in the local Hilton. Once again, they were cautioned about the sun and the lack of water, and instead of continuing by camel, they were flown to Abu Dhabi, their animals following in a truck. Once here, they took a last trip into the desert, the camels were given away and the Englishman took up his post with the Embassy.

After he had told me his story I had said, "I'm envious. I must tell you that."

"Of what?" asked his young wife, meaning no harm. "Of crossing the desert in a lorry and a plane?"

And I thought while driving of how the large attempts at adventure are now so unavailable to us, and how our small attempts at it pass unrecognized. For the next quarter hour, on my last day in Arabia, I tried to remember the words to this poem:

> Mr. T.
> > bareheaded
> > > in a soiled undershirt
> his hair standing out
> > on all sides
> > > stood on his toes
> heels together
> > arms gracefully
> > > for the moment
> curled above his head.
> > Then he whirled about
> > > bounded
> into the air
> > and with an *entrechat*
> > > perfectly achieved
> completed the figure.
> > My mother
> > > taken by surprise
> where she sat
> > in her invalid's chair
> > > was left speechless.
> Bravo! she cried at last
> > and clapped her hands.
> > > The man's wife
> came from the kitchen:
> > What goes on here? she said.
> > > But the show was over.†

† William Carlos Williams, "The Artist."

The driver had interrupted these reflections by pointing out a newly built bedouin village. Then he read from the sign: "Forty villas, two schools, six employee houses, twelve shops, one clinic, one reservoir, one mosque." They were a gift from the Ruler.

I looked at the long row of low buildings. They seemed abandoned: flat, unbroken surfaces with nothing but the empty world surrounding them, and no blade of grass as far as the eye could see. I suggested that we drive into the village.

"It used to take us five days," said the driver, "to get from this distance to Abu Dhabi, then five days there to get provisions, then five days to get back." He laughed. "Ten years ago! And now it takes an hour and a half."

We drove next to one of the buildings, and, as though pulled from some source below, the car was immediately embedded in the sand.

It was the sudden reality of the sand's power that surprised me. I had walked on it, ridden out on it; it was always there, it surrounded everything. The new cities tried to deny its existence—tried, at least, to obscure it. But it had the force of an ocean.

It was midday. No one came out of the houses towards us; no car streaking by on the highway noticed our predicament. A lone camel in the distance hurried off across the flatlands with a strange urgency, as though late for an appointment. We tried to force a piece of wood under the tires, we tried a fragment of corrugated metal. Nothing worked. The car had gotten more deeply embedded; its motor groaned, its wheels spun uselessly. The driver grew sullen and began to wave away my attempts to help. Gone was his laughter about the hour and a half it now takes by car to cross the desert. Then he walked across the sand towards the highway.

A woman heavily veiled in black came out of one of the houses, billowed alongside its wall and disappeared into the gate of the house next door without looking in the direction of the marooned car. Nothing else moved. The twelve shops were empty; so were the two schools; the clinic was closed. The air conditioners attached to the houses had begun to rust. Soon the driver reappeared inside a Land-Rover driven by some bedouins.

Silently they got out and attached the ropes to the car. The ropes snapped when they tried to move it. Then they tried again. A breeze had come up and they covered their faces with their head scarves. Again they tried. We pushed the stranded car, the Land-Rover pulled it, now in reverse, and the car was gradually eased out of the sand and dragged to a firmer place. I watched the driver reach into his billfold, and in the quiet I could hear the crackle of money as he handed it to the bedouins, shattering the fabled rule of the desert that no reward is ever offered or accepted for help; that water is to be given even to an enemy. The man taking the money inclined his head away and quickly secreted it into his robe. Then the car doors shut and their car turned back onto the road.

Now on firmer ground, we drove to the highway. I looked back at the village, its cement houses waiting to be filled with the new life that prosperity had made possible, that prosperity had urged on the bedouins who had come there in so recent a past, with nothing at all; had come there because there was nowhere else. Soon it was no larger than a collected caravan; then a truck obscured it. Then it was gone and there was only sand.

Chapter Seven

IRAN

Everyone comes now to the Middle East hat in hand. Pan American's around-the-world flight touches down each evening in Tehran, the huge 747 cylinder of Western civilization depositing shuffling crowds gaga from too much time in the air; then it raises its wings out of reach, taking America with it, taking rare, medium, taking well-done steaks, and contoured seats and undubbed films and earnest stewardesses with open smiles (*"There* you go." *"Sorry* about that"), dressed without a wrinkle, carrying them on to Karachi, to Delhi, the blue globe on its white tail growing ever smaller as the ex-passengers grimly face the dark, moneyed Middle East, wondering as they line up, red-eyed, their passports in hand, how in the world all this came about.

Inside every briefcase there is a scheme. They come to sell planes, seven planes, for the cost of one billion two hundred million dollars. They come to sell industrial complexes—the accourtrements, that is. More modestly, they also come to sell tractors and trucks. They bring bright catalogues and readied invoices. But all is not serene. The planes, it seems, will need the assistance of the United States Air Force to operate them. The industrial computers have three-pronged plugs, it is discovered later, and the wall socket can only accommodate two. The tractors rust in vast fields, disintegrating under the vengeful sun. They cannot be transported to their faraway destinations. The transport trucks (in primary colors), giants with forty pairs of wheels and block-long trailers, remain at the docks. The roads and bridges of Iran would buckle beneath them. "I firmly believe that we will have joined the ranks of the major industrialized powers by 1990,"[*] the Shah has said. But I see that you have gotten the idea of what all those foreigners are doing there.

It is reasonable to be kind to unknown cities, to imagine that there are corners of interest waiting to reveal themselves with time. In Istanbul, the pervasive melancholy finally particularizes it and makes it interesting, so

[*] *Al-Ahram*, Tehran, May 1976.

down-at-heel, so reduced, perched where only a great city should have been. Cairo gradually assumes a connection to Upper Egypt, and then to ancient Egypt because of the Nile, and so it enters the imagination and is enhanced by the imagined atmosphere. But Tehran, bereft of beauty, is unrelieved by sea or river. Nothing is promised. There are no fragments of past Persia, and the few elements of future Iran are undistinguished. There is a large, modern, turbaned arch as you drive into town, standing on the flatlands waiting to have its picture taken. There is not a tree. There is not a pushcart. Soon the city will creep to its unlovely feet and beyond. Blue—Heavenly Blue—morning glories, the variety banned in America because its seeds were being ground up for a high, scramble down the center of the highway. In the streets, the chaos is complete, the cars forming and re-forming into graphs of anxiety. There are no sidewalk cafés to give frames to the human animation. There are no coffeehouses or tearooms. There is no charm.

Tourists are reduced to a frantic search through their guidebooks for something to grasp, ending up, ironically, underground, in the vault of a bank. There, behind a proper steel bank vault door, for two dollars, the customers can gape at the crown jewels displayed in glass cases pierced by spotlights in the hush of a darkened room. "You know which ones I'd steal?" says someone as though anyone would care. "*I'd* steal . . . let me see . . ." And then this simple lady in the pantsuit ponders a coronation tiara set with 1469 diamonds, 36 emeralds, 34 rubies and 105 pearls. "Those!" she says in triumph, pointing to a more modest set of emerald earrings in the shape of strawberries. "Huh?" says her companion, "Which ones, honey?" Then he eyes the Sea of Light diamond, the biggest pink diamond the world has ever seen, a portion of the Great Table diamond—the names are stupendous—a partner of the Koh-i-noor, the Mountain of Light diamond.

"Will you look at that!" he says to her, and they press in close to the case, too close for the guard, who walks over and whispers them away. These stones have crossed dangerous borders, have survived assassinations, court deceits, and Mogul emperors, and now the Sea of Light sits solemnly in a bank vault on white velvet, back under the earth again.

"How much is it worth?" the man asks, returning to the guard in a man-to-man aside. "I mean *really* worth?" The guard shrugs. It is his job to protect, not to appraise. He points to the catalogue. It says: "We are often asked as to the value of a specific item, and we regret to say that we are no wiser in this respect than the questioner. We can only describe the total value of the treasury as immeasurable."

There are emerald epaulettes and ruby cups and turquoise rays of sun. There are gold decanters and jade ladles and a room-long robe embroidered with pearls. There is every jewel you have heard of, only larger, fashioned into something that never crossed your mind: jeweled rings for horses' tails, jeweled pistol holders, jeweled quivers. It is appropriate that this treasure is the pride of Iran (the archaeological museum is a tumbledown place, its artifacts neglected). There is something about jewels that suggests, well, immortality. And besides, as you draw closer to them you begin to see an entire universe of your own reflections shimmering back at you. They are the ideal luminous symbol for a country under the rule of someone whose title is so ablaze with refractions: His Imperial Majesty Mohammed Reza Pahlavi Aryamehr Shanshanshan of Iran, those two bewildering words towards the coda meaning "the light of the Aryans, the king of kings." "My reign has saved the country and it's saved because God was beside me. I mean, it's not fair for me to take all the credit for myself for the great things I've done for Iran. Mind you, I could. But I don't want to, because there was someone else behind me. It was God. Do you see what I mean?"†

"I *cannot bear* this need to achieve," says a woman at a horse-jumping competition. Her sons are contenders for the main prizes. She is sleek as all get-out. Her sunglasses even have designer's symbols on the earpieces. She has employed a person with videotape equipment to record the events in which her boys will compete. She has seen my cameras. Yes, I say, I will take some pictures of her sons, and, having nailed that one down, she is about to go over and gossip with some friends near the clubhouse.

"Your husband," I say before she can get away, "is, I understand, an industrialist."

"Yes, yes," she answers absently. "He employs twenty thousand people. But he *can't* get them to work."

"But you spoke of ambition."

"That's just *it*. His employees learn their jobs, and then within a year they try, *they* try to open factories of their own. They want huge bank accounts! So they open their little factories upstairs from where they live, with their brothers, their sisters, their wives. And it all goes wrong. They don't know what they're doing. *Misplaced* ambition! Those," she says with pride, "are my two sons."

She points to one middle-sized and one small boy. Each of them is on a splendid horse, the manes braided with ribbons. It was the Persians who brought the horse, almost four thousand years ago, into western Asia. The Babylonians, the Egyptians, the Greeks had never before seen such an animal.

"Do take their pictures," she says seductively, pushing her sunglasses up on the bridge of her nose. "I'm so nervous about them. Look how beautifully they ride. They want so much to win."

Later, after the competition (both sons had won many of the more important ribbons), and after the videotapes had been taken, and after the press photographers had been persuaded to send her copies of their pictures, she

† Oriana Fallaci, *Interview with History*.

passed me by without a word. The press photographers' photographs would be better than mine anyway. Their cameras were larger.

It is a complication being rich in Iran. When there is so much money to be spent, it is wearying to spend it all at home. Either you must go abroad or you must arrange for the best that is abroad to be sent to you. Decorators arrive from France to do up the new houses built to the north in the hills above Tehran where the cooler breezes are coaxed to blow. The plots are small—some seven hundred meters or so—and even at the amazing prices, the houses have to be built near each other for lack of available land. Sometimes there is a pool; almost always there is a view. And every now and then the architect designs a house in a Persian motif. But there is a tendency towards things in the French taste: Louis Quinze and Seize, when it is good, is imported from France with a customs duty of 300 percent. Inside, upstairs, there is no sense of the seraglio. There are canopied beds with little pleats; there are tapestries where maidens in big skirts frolic with lambs, watched, in the distance, by immobilized shepherds. At dinner there are grapes from Fauchon; there is a little crock of mustard discovered, through a network of international connoisseurs, at a shop off the King's Road. There is a stylishness in dress and manner that is reminiscent of Rome, the Western equivalent of all this. Fancy Italians come frequently to mind, though they seem frivolous in comparison to their equivalents in Tehran. But there is a similar lack of social concentration here, a similar self-conscious parading, a similar glance round the room: people are regarded, appraised, catalogued and dismissed—unless their credentials are unavoidably superior. Everything is skin deep. No one has the time or inclination to bother with more. The Iranians get up in the morning at around six and get home from their offices at around eight at night and they are in bed two or three hours later. They are planning, they are acquiring, they are accumulating.

"Not that I'm interested in that sort of thing any more," says an Iranian gentleman at a dinner, trim and beautifully groomed. He is talking to an Englishman across the table. The Englishman has been politely turning the conversation around to the subject that interests him most: selling cottons to the man opposite him. "But how much," continues the Iranian in an offhand manner, "how much, for example, would bolts of percale run? In plain white."

His *in plain white* has shown his hand. The Englishman brightens.

"In plain white?" he repeats, having sat through three courses waiting for this moment. "Well, I suppose we *could* do them for you in plain white instead of the colored cloths we've been selling to Western Europe. *Plain white's* what we sell to the *Saudis*." And in one stroke he has managed to put down the Iranian (they do not wish to be confused with Arabs) and to push his more expensive materials, while maintaining the surface politeness that has effectively masked the intentions of the British for centuries.

"I think he's awfully attractive," says a beautiful Iranian publicity agent to her friend a seat or two down, motioning towards the man who has now learned that the Saudis order plain white.

"You're absolutely mad," says the friend, turning idly to look, and then turning back.

"Like Marlon Brando, I mean. Not regular features. Something different," persists the publicity woman.

"Well, have it your way. Now *I*"—and here she lowers her voice—"I'd like to know who *he* is. He looks like *some*body."

I feel my ears redden because she is referring to me, and I try to seem to be concentrating on what the woman to my left is saying about the servant problem.

"You're absolutely mad," says the publicity woman, getting even. They are both studying me. I am cloaked in paranoia.

"I guess you're right," says the other woman. "I'd thought . . . well, *no*. He isn't anybody."

And they turn their attention elsewhere.

The women's dress is understated; their jewelry is no threat to the crown jewels. The men have all seen the best tailors. Their sport cars are parked outside. Their servants are treated like servants; they are summoned and dismissed. The glossier Iranians might want the patterned sheets, the good grapes, the fast cars from the West, but they do not long for that equality business.

Twenty years ago most of the world barely knew where Iran was located. Was it in South America? On some of the brochures it still says boldly, IRAN, and then, in parentheses, Persia. The name was changed in 1935 by the Shah's father, an army sergeant who led a coup d'état in 1921. Iran, from "Aryan," the people of Indo-European origin who inhabited the Persian Empire, a land under Cyrus stretching from Libya and Egypt in Africa to Macedonia in the north, across the Caucasus through Samarkand and into India. Now, once again, there are riches, and the rich Iranians go abroad for clothes, for skiing, for health cures, trailing their Asiatic elegance to Europe. Their manners are so courtly, so many of them are so aristocratic and good-looking, and their attitude towards the monarchy is so deferential (the Empress is referred to only as Her Highness in those frequent conversations in which she appears) that the atmosphere cries out for barons and countesses and marquises. But there are none. Any Persian who happened to have had the name Pahlavi was required to change it when the last shah assumed the name. There would be only one family line as king of kings. "King of Kings, a Persian, the son of a Persian, and Aryan of Aryan stock." This is what Darius had written on his own tomb almost five hundred years before Christ, defeated by Alexander the Great. The country goes back, way back in time, and there is a tradition of royalty mixed with reverence: somehow God is implicated in it. We are unaccustomed to it now.

"The Shah even regulates the weather," said an American as we were leaving that dinner. "He keeps the tribes from grazing their goats on the hills. Up until now the hills were bare. Now they're covered with vegetation. The vegetation brings rain clouds. Now *that's* power." And with that, we all went home.

Photographs of the Shah are everywhere, as ubiquitous as the *Daily News* on the New York subway. They are not the usual formal portraits of the current person in charge of the country that prevail in the rest of the Moslem world. Featuring one or more members of the royal family, they more closely resemble stills from various films made by this enterprising group. There seems to be no end to them. One wonders how the family ever found time to get anything else done, to govern, to travel, to do the simplest errand. They pose, and then they pose again. Here is the Shah alone, sitting at a desk signing a document—this one cleverly in the window of a pen shop —and here he is in the uniform of what appears to be the Iranian Boy Scouts. Now he is a soldier—but no, I am mistaken, soldiers do not wear epaulettes. Here he is a skier ready to take on a dangerous slope, and there he stands in a business suit, clouds scudding past him as he waves, uneasily, for the ground underneath him is as curved as the top of a globe—*our* globe, I presume. Now the Empress appears. Relatively jewelless, she sits in front of some venetian blinds, her hands together, her lovely long fingers intertwined. And there she is, sitting on a throne richly encrusted, her neck encircled by very large gems. On another wall, now in a grocery, is the Crown Prince, smiling broadly as only a thirteen-year-old can smile while wearing a silk waistcoat, with the best of everything waiting in the wings. And here is a palace room, with the entire family gathered together again, all of them wearing royal velvet robes and regal expressions. At the Intercontinental Hotel, the Shah and the Empress appear in a large oil painting, life-size next to one of the sofas, giving the impression that the ill-assorted group milling about might be their friends waiting for their host and hostess to arrive with the canapés.

The effect is, finally, that you think you know them, you keep wondering whether you have just seen the Empress pass you in the street. So used to her face is the general public that they have taken it and made it theirs. The women have become their queen. Their eyes are tilted ever so slightly upwards with the heavy use of makeup; their cheekbones have been aided with cosmetics; their hair is at once thick and brownish, and they wear the same abstracted look—a royal look, one might say. In any one day, the Empress will appear several times even in the English newspapers (which, here, are more like press agent's releases), shaking hands, signing documents, spreading goodwill. If it is true that the King of Persia is the only ancient ruler— ancient, as in the Pharaohs—still reigning, then this constant exposure to the royal family of Iran is possibly only a twentieth-century equivalent to the homage paid in Darius' day when the King of Persia was *the shadow of God upon the earth.*

I had an appointment for drinks with the parents of a friend. I had not yet met them. "Our house is near the Austrian Ambassador's residence," said the mother over the phone in beautifully accented English, "on Fareshteh Avenue. Any driver will know the street."

I looked at my map. It was in German and I was lucky to have gotten one. Maps are not readily available. Perhaps it is because the city is growing so quickly, in such a haphazard way. The map said only Farschidstrasse. "Fareschid Street, near the Austrian Embassy," I said to the doorman, hoping he would untangle it when he repeated it to the driver. When I am given an address, I frequently receive an image of the place indicated. It is so detailed that I even imagine the side of the street on which the house will be located, filling in the architecture and the surroundings as I go along. No matter how frequently I am misinformed, these images are accurate just often enough for me to oblige them, lunatic as it seems. In this case, I clearly saw the Embassy (high walls, sentry guards, somewhere on an incline). Farschid, Fareshteh: it would reveal itself as we drove along.

Immediately we turned into a monumental traffic jam. Traffic in Tehran is a way of life. Traffic keeps people at home or it keeps people away from home. The day is shaped around it in an attempt to avoid running into it. Iranians are prevented from dining with friends because they cannot reach each other's houses. Lovers are prevented from sleeping together because they cannot get to each other and get back to where they were. People die at home in their beds, very sensibly, because they cannot be faced with the indignity of dying at a popular intersection. Trips across town take three and four hours. Businessmen rise at five-thirty, groping for their keys in the dark, stealing down the back streets, their emphysematous motors choking in the pre-dawn cold, trying to get to the center of town to find a parking place. Traffic is a substantial entity. It is viewed with some pride, an automated monument to prosperity, a nation's status symbol. The stoplights have been built as large as tractor tires, the red ones principally, with twice the wattage of ordinary stoplights. They remain unobeyed.

"That's a red light," I say as we just miss being slammed into by a car.

"I know," says the driver, his foot still on the accelerator.

"Why don't you pay attention to it?"

"It only tells me whether to expect something from the right or left."

We are now on the smaller streets, with small shops and upstairs industries. The living-room suites for sale are in some kind of shellacked throne style, with bright red velvet cut into heraldic patterns. Crystal chandeliers hang from above, so immense that they graze the armrests with their pend-

ants. There are mirrors reflecting mirrors—is there a national cult of narcissism?—large mirrors, small mirrors, mirror chips for mirrored mosaics, mirrors
still made in the ancient tradition, with closed, decorated doors, intended for
the young bride on her wedding day who opens the lacquered doors (rose-
buds, birds and filigree) to reveal in reverse the first glimpse of the man she is
marrying. The mirror stores reflect and bend and multiply our slow, tedious
passage down the block. We pass bread shops, with ovens in the window and
fresh, unleavened bread, like oblong tractor seats, set outside to dry in the
early evening heat. We pass shops selling things that look like the prizes
promised for poker games at amusement parks; shops filled with fluorescent
light, the circular ones hanging in the window like lit wreaths, the long ones
tied up like lit wheat sheaves, all of them casting a gloomy light as the
mercury streetlamps flicker on dimly and evening approaches. I try not to
look at my watch.

There are small canals running next to the sidewalks, now dry. Water,
precious in Iran, used to come gushing through them at certain hours
throughout the city, for the washing. Dishes would be brought out and
scraped into them, and near the university whores were known to dip into
them between clients. Now people in Tehran have sinks—most people, that
is—and the canals are used mainly to wash the cars. The cars, the cars! We
begin to form lanes where no lanes had ever been intended. Back on the
boulevards we begin a fourth, a fifth lane. In a moment we are on the sidewalk; now we are back in the street. We have terrorized pedestrians and motorists alike. The driver remains unconcerned.

Policemen are unable to tame the traffic; they are matadors in the midst
of a stampede. In addition to the private cars, there are both private and
public taxis and strange, eerily empty buses, routed, it would seem, on un-
popular rides. These private taxis are unmarked. There is no way to tell
them from ordinary cars without trying to flag them down. They serve as jit-
neys, taking as many passengers as they can squeeze in. People line up along
the sidewalks and streets shouting their destinations to the passing cars with
desperation. The drivers of the unmarked taxis incline their heads to the
right to listen as they cruise along, waiting for some sound that might be
significant. Along the curbs there is a chorus of the hopeful. If the driver
hears an address along his route, he will stop just long enough to permit the
passenger to climb in and pull his or her bundles inside. Then he drives off,
the photograph of a grim-faced baby bobbing just underneath his rearview
mirror, the driver's head still inclined starboard, still driving slowly. There is
something obscene in the choreography, the driver-passenger seduction: in
the hawking of destinations, the thrill of the stopped car, the opened door,
the disappointment and anger of those rejects left behind.

A policeman comes over to us. We have stalled behind a cement mixer.
In Lagos, the policemen carry whips to bring the motorists in line. Their
new-rich traffic is on a par with Tehran's. So exasperated is the policeman

with our driving, our creating lanes, that he is unable to speak properly. He stutters, his hand shakes, he writes out our ticket so that it is illegible. The driver accepts it wordlessly, with no automatic flinch, no apology. When the policeman leaves us to reluctantly face his traffic, the driver does not deign to look at the ticket. We pull away from the cement mixer, he takes his hands briefly off the wheel and tears the ticket in half. Then he tears the halves in half, throwing the pieces, in a graceful upward motion, out of the car window, where they dance in the moonlight. It is night. We proceed. But we do not know where we are going.

"You said Fareschid, right?"

"The Austrian Embassy," I say, now avoiding the name.

"Austrian?" he says. It seems to be a word unknown to him.

I ask him to inquire. He calls out of the window to a passing pedestrian. The pedestrian shrugs and walks on. We are now climbing towards the foothills of the snowcapped mountains surrounding the city. He asks someone else. The name of the street has undergone another transformation. No one knows anything about it. "The Embassy, the Embassy," I say without hope. He rolls down the window and asks again. "Australian?" says someone. "Up, up," says someone else who has no idea. I am traveling on the *Flying Dutchman* of Persia awaiting Judgment Day. I ask to stop at a pharmacy. A pharmacy seems somehow serious. "Are you sick or something?" he asks, turning around briefly to study me with the large eyes of southern Asia. "No, I am not sick," I say. "I want to find out how to get where we're going. We could have flown from Athens to Istanbul in all this time." "Istanbul?" cries the driver as I go into the store.

I question the druggist, who does not know, and then I ask for a telephone directory.

"A *telephone* directory?" he says. It sounds like an imitation of Edith Evans in *The Importance of Being Earnest*.

"Information," I say, now half mad. "I need to know where I am going!"

He looks at me with a puzzled expression, takes down the details and calls information. He talks, listens, laughs. Then he hangs up. The name I am looking for is too common. There are three pages of them. They cannot go through them all to find the one on Fareschid Street or on Farschid or on Fareshteh. *We are not computerized*, they had said. *Do you think this is America?* It was then that he had laughed.

I was again in the back seat like some irregular parcel that would remain undelivered. Why had I not thought to bring the telephone number? Why had I made the appointment in the first place with these strangers? Why had I not written the address carefully, phonetically? I was strangling in a suit with a vest. The driver's mind had left him; he began to babble. He was asking everyone who passed for some nonexistent street. They thought he was soliciting them. Or they thought he was soliciting them for me. We

were in front of an embassy: there was a sharp incline. High walls, a pair of sentry guards . . .

"Just up the street," they said in unison. The driver answered that we had already been up the street several times. One of the guards said, "Follow me," and he led us, as though the car was on a leash, to the door of the house.

"The traffic!" said the wife, making it easier for me.

"I was afraid of this!" said the husband, trying to be agreeable. "I'd thought of sending my own driver but he was caught in traffic at the other end of town."

It was two hours later than our appointment. Now it was eight o'clock and I had to be back for dinner in the center of the town we could now see shimmering beneath us below the hill. We walked into the house.

I see the ten minutes I spent with these supremely elegant people in a blur of golden objects, oriental carpets and apology. Carpet after carpet stretched throughout the rooms, carpets suitable for magic-carpet rides above fabled places; carpets on top of carpets, kaleidoscopes contracting, expanding; opulent gardens of color edging vast monochromatic fields; small geometric patterns, hypnotic with their woven arithmetic, against calm prayer rugs meant for meditation. I rattled the ice in my drink, looking past polished objects and wooden surfaces glinting in the lamplight, towards these two people (had I dreamed them? Was I still in the back seat of the car roaming the never-ending streets?), white-haired, smiling across at me. They, polite as diplomats, told me that I was always welcome to return. And I, putting my glass down, standing to leave, assured them that I would be back. But I never had the chance again. They went to the Caspian coast and I went south, and after those ten minutes in that magical house I left to face the long drive back.

In Isfahan, trucks go by piled high with carpets; carpets roll out of stores onto sidewalks; they hang from balconies overlooking blast furnaces where metals are being joined. Sometimes you see a carpet stretched out—just as you heard you would—across a street under the traffic, the wheels of everything passing above it, ageing as rapidly as an escapee from Shangri-La. *Old carpet*, they will say one week hence in the dimness of the bazaar, *very* old, and it might end up a month later, cherished, on the parquet floor of a five-room apartment in the Marais, its secret intact.

Secrets are what it is all about: secrets, surprises, things not quite defined, equivocal, alluring. People have always come to the Middle East for this, before the oil became a larger power than everything else. Isfahan has accumulated a legend as a place of almost transcendental beauty because of the architectural wonders scattered throughout the city.

The mosques and palaces are not genetically connected to what surrounds them; instead, they refer to each other. Across the bleak rooftops of a provincial town that was once the capital of Persia, they seem to synthesize all of the Islamic past Persia has known. The ruins of Persepolis tell of a country too long dead. But the faience domes of Isfahan create a haunting chorus of a more recent past. If, as legend tells us, all Persian music is based on the song of the nightingale, then the chorus high above the rooftops of this town would be that sound. The only pity is that we cannot hear it. But when you close your eyes, tilting back in your chair in the sunlight, the turquoise of the domes remains under your lids, shifting and turning and beckoning.

These sudden wonders are the great pleasure of the Middle East. A minaret will rise as you turn a corner, as though you have caused it to come alive. A dome, somewhere in the distance, will catch your eye, brilliant in the sunlight that falls without reflection on the surfaces surrounding it. Just beyond a corner where someone walks by carrying a tray of dripping beef hearts and livers, past the rueful dealers in rusting locks, or keys, or acetate kerchiefs, an incline will take you up a flight of steps to a small square where people lounge and barter, and beyond the gate—a ticket taker's booth appropriately preparing you for its theatricality—is the Friday Mosque, the Masjid e-Johmeh, perhaps the most extraordinary and atmospheric building in all of Islam. And it was this way that St. Peter's must have startled the visitors to Rome before Mussolini pulled down the quarter surrounding it to give it a proper imperial approach. But such lofty settings diminish great architecture, making too much of it, extracting awe when awe would have been willingly given.

On the main square of Isfahan, the Royal Square, also known more poetically as the Image of the World, the Naqsh-e Jahan, the great buildings bordering it are kept at arm's length by the neat formal park in the square's center, by the rectangular boulevard flanking the park and by the absence of street life or cafés that characterize and give life to its Byzantine counterpart, the Piazza San Marco. It was not always so. When the Naqsh-e Jahan was the center of the capital at the turn of the seventeenth century, the king of all Persia could watch from the balcony of his palace as caravans rolled by and set up tents. The square was covered with sand for polo matches; executions were performed on it. In the evening there were puppet shows and storytellers and tents of dark ladies. Now, having formalized it, having straightened out and manicured its edges and organized the façades, cleaning and polishing it into a soulless respectability, no one lingers, visitors are aware immediately that they are walking across a historic focus of Iran and hurry to the entrances of the mosques, and local people cross quickly to get to the other side of it and to disappear into the bazaar where the life is.

After Shah Abbas had claimed Isfahan as Persia's capital and made it prosper, the Afghans captured it; then it was reclaimed by an Iranian general. He transferred the capital to Mashad, leaving it to deteriorate into a small town with great monuments. But now: "The second phase of the expansion program of the Isfahan steel complex will be more gigantic than the first one, and the third one will be even greater, leading to an annual production of about ten million tons. Isfahan will probably become a major industrial center on a global scale."‡ And so history is not through with it.

I had been staying at the Shah Abbas, one of the seven wonders of the hotel world, so elaborate, so large and imperial in design that it is just this side of being included in the list of the town's major monuments. With gracious ceremony, I was thrown out. No one can stay at the hotel more than a few days. There are always new arrivals or state visits. A morose group assembles in the lobby in the morning, awaiting with fear the calculation of their bills; a new group waits a few meters away, near the doors, bright faced with enthusiasm, eager to sign the registers. One of the sadnesses of travel is the realization of how quickly one is replaced, and it is difficult not to stretch this into a larger application if one is given to brooding.

But I made friends checking out with a young couple in a similar predicament. The desk clerk, a jolly man (in Iran, unlike its neighboring countries, a smile will usually get you a smile) had just written my name, for my amusement, in Farsi. The Persians originally used the Aramaic aphabet, but after the Moslem conquest their language was written in Arabic script, and Arab words were added to the Persian. In its zeal to purify the Persian language and make the country unmistakably Aryan, the present regime is trying to purge the language of its foreign elements, a great difficulty, since less than half the population is genuinely Persian. The rest of the Aryans are composed of two million Arabs, ten million Azarbaijanis, four million Kurds and two million Baluchis, in addition to smaller ethnic groups. All of them have been denied the use of their languages.

"No," said a voice near me, "he's got it wrong. It's *de* Combray, not *di*, which is what he's written."

I looked up to find an American with, if I remember correctly, a plump Asiatic mustache.

"I speak Farsi," he said to reassure me. "I used to go to school here." Then he proceeded to rewrite my name in what was presumably the correct phonetic spelling. I thanked him. The girl with him had eyes the color of the turquoise domes for which Isfahan is so justly famous.

"Your eyes," I said, unable not to say it soon after the introductions were made, "the color, I mean, they're . . ."

"They're glass," she said.

And so the girl with the turquoise eyes (were there other contact lenses

‡ The Shah of Iran's speech during a tour of the Aryamehr Steel Complex, Isfahan, January 1976.

for other cities?) and her Farsi-speaking companion and I became acquaintances—traveling acquaintances. The man's ability with the language
amazed the shopkeepers and prevented them from making the side com-
ments they had grown over the years to cherish. We picked up other acquaintances along the way. Soon we were a band of seven or eight at meals,
during which he translated, ordered and generally officiated. In the modest
restaurants of Isfahan, utensils are brought in a glass of water, napkins come
to the table in a cup, drinking water is served from a whiskey bottle; you eat
your food with a tablespoon and your fingers, a halved raw onion is auto-
matically put down next to your plate, and the sweet made with pistachios
and nougat served at the end of the meal is called *gaz*.

If we did not arrange to meet somewhere, we would run into each other
anyway. Everyone discussed elaborate plans for further travel: on to Kabul,
to Samarkand, through the Khyber Pass to the Hindu Kush. Each place
name was more exotic than the next. They would immerse themselves in
Asia, far from civilized places. They would live with the natives to better
understand them. I was skeptical. I began to think up ways to be alone. It is
not easy to remain alone. It seems to provoke irritation in others, who take
it as a judgment against them. Or it is looked on as an ailment. Or it is considered just unfriendly. Perhaps it is all of those things.

I returned to the Friday Mosque. It would remain with me long after I
left Iran. *Iran*, someone will say, or *Persia*—the more beautiful word—and
through the wind tunnel of images, I can see quite clearly the Masjid e-Johmeh, through a maze of arches; arches within arches, with workmen weaving
through them, restoring them, like woodland creatures, the light filtering
through the dust so that it seems to be a rising mist. The original building
was constructed in the 800's and this part of Isfahan was known as Yahu-
diyeh, where the Jews had settled. The facing of the mosque had been
ripped away in the twelfth century to be used for fuel when the city was under siege. It was again reconstructed; it was again burned. The glazed rooftops
date back to the fourteenth century, when once again the mosque was put
back together, and magpies now walk and skid along the delicate tracery;
then they take flight over the vast courtyard where boys practice their prayers
and gentlemen in business suits pause, solemnly face Mecca and pray, their
jackets flapping in the wind as they kneel. A boy crosses the paving stones
holding the hand of his father, who is blind. He trails his free hand in the
fountain, squints up at the magpies, pauses, but the blind father scolds him,
and he obliges by hurrying on across the courtyard.

"Hey, man, what's happening?"

It was one of the group.

"They screwed up our reservations," he said, "the computer's out of
whack."

"I know," I said. The airline office had been mobbed by irritated clients pushing each other out of the way to learn that no information was available, that the computer had broken down. One of the employees put both his hands up in the air to quiet the crowd; then he picked up and reverentially placed a plastic cover over the great machine. "Raytheon," it said. A powerful cable led into the floor, and beyond it into the bowels of Iran. The crowd stood back from the counter a respectful distance.

"It will work," said the clerk, "when it is ready."

Everyone filed silently out of the office.

"So you see," my acquaintance was saying as the last of the sun hit the dome of the mosque, "if we don't catch a connecting flight getting us to Kabul, we'll never manage to pick up the car that'll get us to . . ."

A continuing documentation of future travel plans is hard to take when you are trying to absorb the present. But this irritation did not seem reason enough for me to have broken unpleasantly with the group. Our relationship came quickly to an end in an unexpected way. That evening as several of us entered the Image of the World in a taxi, we collided with another car. Immediately after the sound and the shock of the crash, there was absolute silence. Then the taxi doors were flung open. "Gotta go," said one. "Can't get involved," "Can't be a witness," said the others. They all scattered like gum wrappers along the sidewalk.

Left alone with me, the driver lowered his head to his hands, still holding the wheel. "I have very bad luck," he said, and tears came to his eyes. "Now it all has to be repaired again. I just *had* it repaired." And he beat his hands against the wheel with anger.

Without having searched for it, without any strong ill will, I now had a good reason not to see any of the group again. The strange thing is that they understood it, and the incident released them from the bond as well.

My return to Tehran was wintry. Harsh winds came down from the north. Iran has been shaped by winds from Siberia and winds from Arabia. It rained, and the streets glistened as traffic oozed along in liquid patterns. At my small hotel, the regular residents got up in full darkness and sang in the hall showers to keep themselves company: mournful ballads about lost love at five-thirty in the chilly morning. In the streets, people warmed themselves around fires in small oil drums. There is a worrying absence of beggars in the streets of Iran, as though the very poor had been removed. There is, of course, no talk of political prisoners and no talk of politics, which is standard when only one political party exists in a country. There is no mention of SAVAK, the Shah's secret police, and no mention of torture or executions. The newspapers are carefully screened to give a proper image. Even news of the Arab world is reported in a remote manner, as though its borders were not pressing hard against Aryan Iran.

The countryside still manages to penetrate the city streets. A lineup of

hens squat on the sidewalk, their feet tied together, and a farmer sits nearby hoping for a sale. A donkey crosses a street unwillingly, weaving through the maze of cars in complete terror, urged on by someone holding a long stick. It seems impossible that any animal could have survived the trek to the center of town. Near the schools—and students are everywhere—young people stream by, biting bright red pomegranates bought from street vendors. Cooked beets are sold in the streets, as big as baby's heads. The flat bread, charred on top by the ovens, is priced by the running foot. There are melons and cucumbers on the carts. The melons are hassock-sized; served in the restaurants, they overrun the plates like beached gondolas. Even the roses seem to be larger here. A gaunt man in mechanic's overalls hurries by with a fuchsia rose in his hand, the rose lighting the bleak avenue like a lantern.

I had set off that day to buy a carpet. It could not be helped. I tried to avoid it, telling myself that I had no need of and could not afford a Persian carpet. But the stores were too provocative, taunting me as I passed with magical patterns in their windows. On the morning I capitulated the electricity in the carpet quarter suddenly went off. The deep stores became caves of darkness lit with small candles. The carpet vendors stood about with their hands behind their backs, rocking on their heels with impatience. The next day, I left.

There are abacuses still, clicking in the small shops around the bazaar, reminding you that you are in Asia. There are tall brass cylinders of water set out on the streets, polished so that they shine like beacons. In these neighborhoods everyone crushes in closer together, more at home here than on the wide boulevards. Men carry piles of goods through the alleys bent in half under carpet covered harnesses, zigzagging across the traffic surrounded by miracles. People from the country pile together at the bus station wearing the bulky clothes and pantaloons of the remote countryside where one-bath villages have received distant word of the country's prosperity. There are heaps of them like left luggage, and they wear the look of the permanently dazed. The cloaked women—here there are no veils—are plump with belongings and babies brought with them on the long journey, their buses stopping and stopping again at check points along the way. Their cloaks have become appendages, reinforcements for their shifting thoughts: they drape the material this way and that; they fiddle with the hems. Now they cover their faces, now they expose them and grip the edges of their cloaks with their teeth.

In the jewelry bazaar a smartly dressed young man enters a shop, and with him are his fiancée, his mother and his sister. They have come to choose a wedding ring. A tray of rings is brought to him. *"You look,"* he says, urging his fiancée, her cloak surrounding her, to the counter. She raises the edge of her cloak to her mouth; then she lowers it. She weaves about herself her own uncertainty. And as she moves about the tray, the two other women move with her. They are three blackbirds hovering over the golden jewelry.

The man backs away, glancing or pretending to glance at an adjoining counter. Now murmuring encouragement and disagreement, the women study the rings. In his beautiful new suit, the fiancé remains apart, knowing that he can afford any ring they choose. Whatever he has done this past decade of his life has been carefully calculated to bring him success. He is not liable to read Gorky, Jack London or Brecht and get himself thrown into the Komité for subversive activities and run the risk of having his nails torn out. His sense of newly prosperous well being is not unpleasant: it lightens him, he has earned it. He eyes the cases of the men's watches, drumming his fingers on the glass. "Have you decided?" he asks. The three women turn to him. "You do it," they say.

He strides over to the counter, studies the tray quickly and thoroughly and picks out a ring without hesitation. "This one," he says, and then, with an imperiousness still new to him, he adds, "and I will have that watch." The salesman obliges, nodding his head deferentially. The women beam. The cloak of the fiancée is now about her shoulders. Her hair is abundant. Her eyes have a slight tilt. She, too, looks like the Empress.

Chapter Eight

ALGIERS

There can be something seriously masochistic in traveling through alien places. The usual series of conventional problems are exchanged for a combination not only different in kind but far more troubling. Airport waits, luggage dispensations, customs scrutinies become convoluted indignities accepted without reciprocal complaint. There is no one to turn to. You have asked for trouble and you have found it. Guns gleam from leather holsters. You are not welcomed. You are prodded to the next step in the process of getting through, getting in. And once entered into the ledgers, once let into the country, once settled into the clanking vehicle taking you to an unfamiliar place, you have further abasements in store. Your name evokes no glimmer of recognition at the hotel. Your reservation has left no trace in the files. Your pleas are but gnats in the scorched, surly air. Such is your arrival in Algiers, and there is more to come.

NON, is what is said at the front desk.

There is a pause.

"But," you say, still not stammering, "the reservation was made a month ago. Are you sure?"

You have not understood your role. There is a look hurled in your direction like the snap of a whip. "I have said that there is no room."

You still stand firmly, postponing bondage. "I'd like your name."

It is a futile gesture. No one is fooled.

"Why? Are you the police?"

"No." Then there is a beat. "Can you propose another hotel?" you ask, backing down in manner, backing away in space.

"Non," says the concierge, now not looking up.

"I'd like to leave my luggage here while I look elsewhere."

You watch another layer of pride disintegrate as he deigns not to hear you. You are a blur with some baggage out on the streets.

You rouse someone napping behind a desk who snarls *complet*, and out again you go, back to the streets under the all-seeing, all-knowing sun, its rays hitting your head like a jackhammer. People brush past you, annoyed to be inconvenienced by the luggage you haul, switching it, then switching it again from hand to hand, the act of rebalancing the weight somehow a comfort, a promise that things will change in your favor.

The banner fluttering across the boulevard says ABAJO IMPERIALISMO, aimed at impressing a Mexican President who rumbles by in a cavalcade of Russian-built limousines. LUCHA ANTI-IMPERIALISMO E ANTI-SONISMO! it says on the next sign strung between the traffic light and the lamppost. The last limousine in the line leaves behind a trail of dust and bits of broken road. No one has watched the display; their bad tempers remain unabated despite such fanfare.

In the shade of a café you order a beer and you grumble, flanked by your baggage and your misfortune. No one much notices you—the only relief of the day—for they sit slouched at their own tables staring too steadily at infinity to care. They cough, they spit, they belch heavily: small static interruptions in their dour concentrations. Sicknesses never located in your neighborhood at home are now available to you at every street corner. If you do not choose to inhale them you can tilt your smudged beer glass to your lips and approach them in that way. The bartender comes out wearing a palette of stains on an apron and tells you that you must leave. Everyone must leave: it is the law. Cafés in Algiers close for an hour at three in the afternoon and that is that. You gulp the rest of your beer, conscious that no one around you has been drinking anything. They are there to sit the hours away and stare at God.

Go then. Trudge on. This is Algiers, once France's shimmering jewel in the Mediterranean. The brightest of white cities rising from the sea, set against the lush chain of hills beyond. "A diamond set in an emerald frame," it says in Arab lore. You pick up your things, your eternal foreigner's baggage, moving down the road, up one alley and down the next, only gradually discovering that you have finally come to a place that has no room for you, no room for you at all. It is a concept so alien to the traveler's sensibility that it becomes a curiosity unto itself, an unexpected artifact among known rules. The reason there is no room in Algiers is that every inch of the place is occupied by Algerians themselves who cannot find a place to live. Hotels are not for visitors. You are in the way. You are of no use to anybody.

No one pushes, no one haggles, no one points; they do not tell you their grievances, clutch at your sleeve, pluck at their organs, implore you to buy. Their eyes do not scan your person or offer you with a seductive glance some untold wonders waiting in store. You are barely acknowledged. *Go!* says someone on Ché Guevara Boulevard—once the Boulevard de la Répub-

lique. *Go to the edge of the town.* You will find there a new hotel. A hotel as large as an airport. The biggest hotel in the world. Business men go there to plot investments, to plan industries. Go there, and if you are not too late, you will find a room. It will cost you the earth.

Night approaches, the mauve light of the Mediterranean offering solace to the hard-worked hills from Spain to Syria. The jagged heat goes, releasing springs of swallows to spiral and soar above the towns. You cannot pause to reflect. Once found, the hotel looms like a fortress in the Sahel hills above the city, constructed, it seems, for a race of giants. It is a thing apart, made to show off might, jutting out from the hills like a colossal fist. Its vast halls echo with the somber conversations of organizational people. The elevators play taped music from the forties. Outside, there is an unfinished swimming pool waiting for tons of cement, a lakeful of water and an Olympic team to fill it. Inside, there are unplugged television sets waiting for a cable. The windows are sealed against the Algerian night. The air conditioning is on full blast at some unalterable Arctic setting. The restaurant is closed. The *bureau de change* will be open for one hour and one hour only the following morning. You fall onto your bed muttering, startling yourself because of your incoherence, waiting for a sleep which now will not come at all.

It was said after the eight-year revolution severing Algeria from France in 1962 (two hundred and fifty thousand Algerians were killed, five hundred thousand were wounded, two million lost their homes) that France gave away the house but saved the furniture. The furniture here is the Saharan oil, and France has remained its major investor. The house that France "gave away" can be falsely considered a piece of property abandoned by the masters and left to rot in the hands of the servants. More accurately, the natives took back a place enriched by the Europeans and then found themselves wondering how to care for it. Over a million *colons* had settled in Algeria. They built, educated and tyrannized it, making it their own. They thought of themselves, finally, as Algerians. Now they are gone. About thirty thousand *pieds noirs* remain, and twice that number are temporarily in Algeria as technicians or teachers. It is the classic aftermath of independence: how to use it after the enemy has left, and how to redefine the enemy.

FUTUR MOSQUE, announces a sign attached to a disused church on the main boulevard. It will henceforth be known as Ben Badis, which is also the new name of a town in the cereal-growing country once called Descartes. Meanwhile, Descartes, handed around like the Old Maid card, is now the name of a *lycée* formerly called Fromentin. Fromentin surfaces as the name of a small square where he used to set up his easel. The Cathedral of St. Philippe was a mosque before the French came, and is now a mosque again. Everything in Algiers seems to have undergone a series of metamorphoses: the Archbishop's palace is a tourist agency; a statue of an Algerian rebel has replaced a statue of his former enemy, a French *maréchal*. The Palais d'Hiver is office space.

Up and down the streets there are declarations. The bookshop features Marxist literature in its window, the rifle and gun shop has tacked a map of Palestine in 1948 on its wall; MOROCCO IS OUR ENEMY, it says inside a café; ARRIBA CASTRO, it says on a lamppost. The sign "Kiosque de Bonheur" on top of an Algerian fortune teller's booth is heavily stamped with Islamic symbols and the hammer and sickle as well. There are so many conflicting allegiances that it is like watching a weathervane gyrate in a high wind. And there are so many confused hatreds that dark flights of intangible enemies have polluted the air. The mass of unemployed (about a third of the population) trails morosely through the streets or sits listlessly in cafés, as though some unnamed holiday had been declared and it is obligatory to mourn throughout it. Just underneath this fretful exterior, there is a violence unequaled in the Maghreb. It is not only the obvious prevalence of accidents, the swollen lips, bloody bandages, arms in slings, crutches—but, underneath, the sense that something will erupt suddenly to send the sullen atmosphere crashing to pieces. There are too many people out of work, too many hours to kill until nightfall, too many forms to fill out in triplicate, too many strict hours for this and for that, and too many children racing mindlessly through the streets which are redolent with too many drains overflowing.

I would drive to the countryside, to see the land cherished by Camus, Flaubert and Maupassant. *Outside, beneath the terrace, rolled the sea, and the waves of darkness beat the shore. . . . The air was warm, the heavens filled with stars, the nightingales were singing in the plane trees . . .* , wrote Daudet. The problem was to find a car. The automobile agencies were closed, or had moved, or had vanished. I located the lone rental office still open. Without realizing it I was about to have another of the comedy scenes fast becoming endemic to the agencies along my way. The woman behind the desk was extremely beautiful, the kind of beauty one suspects lies behind the triangular veils hooked onto the nose that force Algerian women to resemble goats. Her apricot skin was smooth, her shining teeth were bared in an open smile.

"And when would you bring the car back if I can find one?" she asked.

I stared at her, disbelieving my good fortune. Her voice was soft and her dark eyes had assumed a slight edge of mockery.

"Whenever," I mumbled. I would dedicate my life to her if she would get me out of that city. She must have known it. Her eyelids closed languidly.

"But when?" she asked.

I said, "Saturday."

"Ah . . . *non*, monsieur. We are closed Saturday."

I began to say Sunday.

"*And* Sunday," she continued. "We are also closed Sunday. In any case," she added, rapidly consulting a chart, "there is no car available."

And with that she closed her ledgers on Algeria.

When Boumedienne took control of Algeria in 1965 it was reported that his speech would be covered by television. In a country with so few television sets this was an important event, and the public gathered in cafés and restaurants to watch the man who ousted the revolutionary Ben Bella in a powerful coup d'état. A loudspeaker came onto the screen, then remained on the screen while a disembodied voice gave its speech. There was no face; only the loudspeaker. This lack of definition and the amorphous authority it implied was to determine the atmosphere of the country: a government beyond reach, paired with the Koranic belief that each man should exist completely in himself with no hope meandering towards the mortal future. The combined formlessness has the weight of a mountain. If it was some master-slave relationship I had sensed at the airport in Algiers, I found that none of the weapons naturally available to me were useful. How does a traveler combat oppressive power that says nothing but *I told you no?* He leaves, I suppose, or he succumbs. And he is punished.

I found a cheap room in a hotel appropriately named the Oasis, though there was no water to be coaxed out of the sole faucet in its sink. When the

heat of the day became intolerable, I lay on my bed watching the play of lights that entered the room through the louvered shutters covering the window. A stream of cars passed in miniature across the ceiling; then there were blank spaces, and shadowy figures moved along the lateral wall. No sleep was possible. I would pick up one book and then another. I learned from Braudel that in the 1500's Algiers had been a city of "Berbers and Andalusians, of renegade Greeks and Turks, thrown together pell-mell." Then came the Barbarossas, and with them the Italians; Northern Europeans arrived, the English and the Dutch, and there were Barbary pirates, always preferred by legend. They were ruled by a succession of Turkish criminals whose only concern was accumulating personal wealth. None of the civilized reforms practiced elsewhere, none of the Arts or Humanities or Sciences were ever given a thought. And slaves, *many of them foreigners* kept the streets clean.

When the heat diminished, I walked—or more properly shambled—to the harbor to sit along the railing and watch the boats leave. Marseilles was a night away on a ship, but the fact of reaching France so easily, so quickly, seemed a trick of the imagination. Over a half million Algerians had left since the revolution, hoping to find, in Europe, something undefined; better, in any case, than what they knew at home. They would work for low wages, lower than the Europeans; there they would stir up trouble and resentments and get into brawls, living in squalid communities where only the food was better than it was back home, and the plumbing, and hopefully the women. They would leave on the overnight boats with cardboard suitcases, the beguiling lights of Algiers behind them along the harbor, beckoning all the way up in the hills. Cities at night promise everything, particularly when they are about to be left behind.

An old gentleman stood near me against the railing, picking his teeth aimlessly as he looked out to sea. He muttered something, coughed and continued on his way. Everyone walking along the sea front would glance out at the water, at that wide, nocturnal invitation to Europe. There was a whistle, then a ship's horn, and a small freighter slowly eased away from the dock. I left, walking along the boulevards past the small knots of women who clustered around the jewelry windows, gaping with fascination at the unexceptional gold things displayed there, shaking their heads vigorously to reveal, just under their goat veils, similar gold jewelry on their ears and around their necks. This is their entertainment, I thought, this gold jewelry: their entertainment and their reward. I noticed, in the reflection of the jeweler's window, that I had neglected to shave.

In the fluorescent-lit restaurant there were solitary men with fierce faces turned angrily inwards. I was seated at a table with a young man with longish hair and a mustache who was listening to the waiter recite the menu in a monotonous singsong.

"And a beer!" he called as the waiter retreated with his order.

"In Constantine, where I come from," he confided, "you can't get a beer anywhere except in one restaurant on a Saturday night. And you've got to have dinner there to get it."

"Is that why you're in Algiers?" It seemed a decent reason.

"I've come here *to take a plane.* Ha, I bet that surprised you."

I said that it did.

"I'm going"—and here he lowered his voice—"to Morocco, then to Spain. Morocco is the cheapest ticket."

I asked him why he was going.

"It's not politics, if that's what you think. I don't care about the Sahara."

I said that it wasn't what I'd thought. I thought it was to find work.

He took off his watch, shook it, and put it on again. It was one of those preparations people go through while deliberating whether or not to sprawl the contents of their life onto a stranger's table.

"It's to get away from my family," he said angrily. "I told my mother two nights ago that I was leaving. And then I left. I didn't say goodbye to my father."

I asked him why, now getting interested, forgetting about the waiter who stood impassively next to me reciting the menu.

My table companion now introduced himself as Said; this formality enabled us to continue in earnest.

"My parents wouldn't allow me to marry my girl friend. They prevented it. She wasn't traditional enough; she was too free, she even had a job. They wanted me to marry my mother's sister's daughter, my own first cousin, and she's"—he stabbed his dried veal with a fork—"she's . . . ugly!"

I tried to think of something to say but there was no need.

"I was lucky. I had seen her once on a visit. A lot of my friends don't get the chance. They ask to see photographs." He looked up. "By the way, are you growing a beard? I thought of growing one." He stroked his bare chin.

"No. It slipped my mind to shave. I've seen," I said, "the retouched photographs in the studios along the street."

"My girl friend was beautiful," he said with pride. "I asked my parents to give me some time to think. In the meanwhile, her parents got angry waiting, saying that they turned down two suitors. So they marry her off, she gets pregnant right away, quits her job and that's that."

"Do you ever see her?"

"Sometimes, on the street. But she doesn't say hello because her husband won't permit it."

My food arrived and I looked down at the stark piece of veal lost in the center of the thick plate.

"Why couldn't the two of you just leave?" I asked.

"JUST LEAVE?" He threw down his napkin. "Where would we live?

How would we eat? I give my father half my salary. My brothers and my sisters, all of us, sleep in the same room. Daytime, it's a living room. When we get married we move into our parents' room and they sleep with the children. I've saved a year for this ticket. Just leave! I am *just leaving*." He had pushed his plate away, his food unfinished.

"Okay, okay," I said, "Let me buy you another beer."

He suddenly smiled. "Do you think I'll get a job in Spain?" he asked.

I said I didn't know that much about Spain, but Spain was close to France and that might not be so bad. Then we talked and I was given the obligatory five minutes an eighteen-year-old allows for the other, older person to speak of himself. We said that we would meet again, and I walked back to my hotel to try once again to get some sleep. But it was to be another of the undated nights of insomnia in Algiers.

"I adore these Arabian nights. If only they'd last all day," says a sleek visitor from France wearing a flowered hat, sitting on an improbable vine-covered terrace with the sea in the background. It is in the film *Pepe Le*

Moko, which was made again, in English, as *Algiers*, and once again as a film, with songs, called *Casbah*. During the thirties, the kasbah was synthesized by Hollywood into an image of dangerous glamour. To Westerners, the tortuous streets were a theatrical set, although Le Corbusier considered the kasbah of Algiers a masterpiece. It was built on a ridge above the town, most of it constructed before the late 1800's. The architecture has come from Andalusia, from Turkey, from Venice; the streets are so narrow that the vaultings over them are formed by the rooftops. It was never quite absorbed or understood during the long French occupation. They called the Rue N'Sara—the Street of the Christians—the Rue du Sahara. They called the Street of Honey (Assel), the Street of the Saddle (Selle). But no matter. It is impossible to find your way anyway. The kasbah is crowned by a citadel built by a Turkish corsair in the 1500's, and this entire section of Algiers has remained relatively impenetrable through the centuries—which brings me back to Pepe Le Moko, a jewel thief in the finest cinematic tradition. He managed, in all three films, to remain hidden from the authorities until the last five minutes before the credits. Protected there by the loyalties of the half-breed Gypsy/Arabs inhabiting the sets, he dreamed of Paris unaware that he would be shot pursuing his beloved in the city streets below, to the heavy strains of the March Slav. We have all grown up on such celluloid images of places, believing in them frequently against our will, somehow angry with the place itself when we discover in real life that we were misinformed.

The last Dey of Algiers took refuge in the kasbah and met with a situation more complicated and weighty than Pepe Le Moko's, though with a note of humor. In 1827, after an unpleasant and lengthy dispute concerning a million francs loaned by the Dey to France—to permit them to purchase some corn—the Dey, wanting his money back, not fully comprehending that he had been deceived by the middlemen arranging the loan, met with the French consul. There he struck him in the face with his fan. No apology would do. The French landed, as they seem to do throughout history, and three years later Algiers was theirs.

Once I discovered the kasbah I lost all interest in the rest of Algiers. The narrow streets mount, climbing to the citadel; windows lean out on stilts almost touching each other in the darkness blocking the sky. The heat is wedged out, penetrating only the small squares where there are mosques or the local water supply. The kasbah was built to house twenty thousand Arabs. Now one hundred and twenty thousand live there. Kids rush down the long flights of stairs kicking homemade soccer balls—foam rubber wrapped in plastic bags—invented, as are other toys, out of scraps. Pinwheels are cut book pages, folded and stapled and pinned to a stick. Everything is patched together. Broken eyeglasses are held in place by rubber bands and Scotch tape; shirts and pants are mended, then mended and mended again;

bottle caps become checkers, a sprig of parsley becomes a fly whisk, a once-beautiful Moorish door supports an abandoned stall with a corrugated roof. And the most surprising transformation of all is in the Algerian of the kasbah. Within these walls, underneath the sharp, pervading sense that everyone is alert—a Neapolitan quickness of observation—there is unexpected kindness and consideration. Inside the houses it is cool. Relatives cram the rooms and courtyards and laundry flaps in the rooftop sun, and it would seem like any Mediterranean village perched on a hill. But there is none of the frivolity found in Europe. The perspective reaches, as it does throughout the Islamic world, beyond the moment, beyond the lifetime. It is always there, and it is often interpreted as indifference.

In the tombs of the marabouts, the local saints, women go to pray, to meditate, to gossip. There, unveiled, they whisper privately to the alms box after extracting coins from tied handkerchiefs, asking the saint's help through the brass slot burnished by fingers and coins and lips so that it shines in the near-darkness of the small sacred rooms. As in the city below, the men congregate in the cafés of the kasbah. Everyone knows everyone else, and everyone else's business as well. Finally, after several trips, I established my own café, high above the city, and I tried, there, to extract some truth about the disparity between the once-opulent Europeanized city's hostility and the relative harmony in these cluttered streets above it. It is against my nature to generalize, because my mind cannot encompass all-inclusive perceptions. When I am faced with a wide scenic view, as many others have done I turn my back on it to study something nearby, pleased to know the view is there but genuinely unable to fathom it. Although it is tempting to report that the Algerians are ill at ease and sour in an atmosphere of abandoned French respectability, and that they manage very well in surroundings the colonials never managed to penetrate and thus distort, I am sure that the theory will be disputed by minds far more geared to theory and politics than mine.

There, beneath the café, the Mediterranean shimmered in the afternoon light as I ordered my coffee in faltering Arabic. Then I fidgeted with my photographic equipment, and my notebook, generally arranging my mule's burden on the ground next to me. When I looked up, I saw Said standing at my table. There was no need to question how he had found me at the café, for the law of the kasbah is to see everything and to communicate some of it to interested parties.

"I'm leaving," he said. "I'm really leaving. I've got my ticket!" He fell into the seat opposite me, raking his hand through his hair.

"When?" I asked anxiously, thinking, irrationally, that my plane would never take off, that everyone else would leave.

"Tomorrow. And you?"

"The day after."

"Come with me to the airport. Think of it! A foreigner seeing me off."

"You're crazy," I said. "Have a coffee."

"Look, Morocco," he said, showing me his ticket. "Why do you look like that? *I'm* not worried."

I laughed. "I guess I'm not worried either. I just walk around Algiers with a worried expression."

"We'll have dinner tonight. And beer. We'll celebrate. It's my treat," he said.

"You'd better save it for Spain," I said. "You can buy me dinner in Spain." I saw in his eyes, at that moment (the sea in the background frozen into a silver path stretching to Europe), the look of wild belief reserved for the very young and sometimes exercised by the incurably foolish. It is the gaze of someone who embarks on a clearly doomed love affair. I tried to return a facsimile of that look of unobstructed hope.

Late that afternoon an inexplicable fog enveloped the harbor. The boats suddenly withdrew from the docks, leaving only pinpoints of light suspended in the air. It seemed impossible to experience such oppressive heat at the same time as the melancholy vapors swirled in their wintry way across the sea. I walked back to my hotel. It was Algiers' rush hour. Horns honked without stopping, as they do in all Moslem cities where the sovereignty of the automobile is hailed. I began to recognize certain faces; the city was not as vast and anonymous as it had seemed when I had arrived . . . how long ago? Occasionally men wearing some kind of khaki revolutionary gear would weave through the crowd, a few fezzes, a few berets, an inexplicable albino cloaked in heavy robes, and always the absence of women. At the hotel someone hanging around the front desk wordlessly handed me my key, barely looking up from his writing. I was now a regular, absorbed into the atmosphere of Algiers without a trace. In my room I tried to coax a current of air by opening the shutters but none would come. I thought that I might have a fever. Then I went to the bureau to check my ticket, and assuring myself that I was reserved on a flight leaving in two days, pushed all my mail from the bed to the floor, and lay back in a stupor of heat and perspiration. I had no energy left to plan anything, and no will. I glanced down at the mail I had collected. On the back of a clipping from the New York *Times* fallen on the frayed rug next to my bed, I read the following advertisement:

Come on, people, meet the People people. They're young, they're educated, they've got plenty of money, they live in the right places.

They're moving—upward and onward and outward. They're plugged into what's happening today. They're with it. They're into the new ideas, the new styles, the new ways to enjoy life.

They're out front, leading the pace and setting new trends rolling. They're the quicker-picker-uppers, who pick up on the new thing and make it the big thing. They're now—the mid-seventies—the contemporary scene.*

And I looked up at the ceiling thinking that, after all, I might be better off here in the kasbah. Then I closed my eyes and fell asleep for fourteen hours.

I was awakened by Said knocking frantically at my door. He was suddenly frightened, he said, appearing in great agitation with his suitcase. I blinked at him in the hallway. It was noon. His flight was to leave in two hours. His nervousness signaled mine, although I tried not to show it, and I paced around the room trying to pull myself together, gathering up my passport and money and map. In the street there were no taxis. We searched up and down the block: nothing. Quickly we raced to a taxi stand only to find a line of a dozen people there before us. We fidgeted, we paced; a line of people continued to form behind us, but there were still no taxis. A man got out of a black car, walked over to us, told us that he would take us to the airport and named a price that caused Said to fly into a rage. He said, it is unjust; the driver said, it is my price; I said, we have no choice. Finally we

* Reprinted by special permission of *People* magazine; © 1975, Time, Inc.

settled on a lower price, and, along with it, a half bottle of scotch I had up in my room. He drove us to my hotel and I brought the bottle down. Then we set off for the airport.

"In Morocco, they're concerned with individual pleasures, aren't they?" asked Said. "Like hashish." He was sitting on the edge of his seat, looking apprehensively through the windshield.

"You'll find it all out," I said. "Anyway, hashish is old-fashioned now."

"Spain," he said stuttering, "Es s-pagne. I admire the Spanish. They're austere, I understand."

I agreed. "I admire the Spanish too," I said.

We did get to the airport on time, and Said managed to retain his composure as he went through the investigations of his visa and the long formalities of the inspectors. It was when I was about to follow him into the waiting room that I discovered my passport was missing.

I behaved in the way one behaves, like a marionette gone wild, touching pockets, touching places where pockets might have been with sixteen Shiva hands grasping out at air the way we do when we are falling and there is nothing anywhere nearby to hold us up. And in my mind, as my hands went their ways, I sped through the spectrum of thefts and losses that might have taken place since leaving the hotel. I saw the passport wedged into the back seat of the car, then I saw the passport being removed from my pocket as the driver bent to open the door. The passport resurfaced now at the taxi stop, there, plainly, on the sidewalk. Then the passport fell in slow motion into the great cave in the earth that receives all things that are lost forever.

Oblivious to this spectacle, Said had gone beyond to wait for me, into that neutral gear past the frontier. He had left Algiers. In slow motion, I stopped fumbling. I stood there completely alone. Now, with grief and clarity, I remembered that most of my money and traveler's checks were in the case with the passport. The chaos of the airport blurred around me, dissolved, just as large rooms do during the most perfect moments of a waltz. Only your partner is in focus, moving gracefully, swaying, almost beyond your reach, and way in the background there is the music. I thought: *It is all over now. Now they have me as theirs.*

Obediently I made the proper inquiries, filled out the proper forms, reported my loss in triplicate to the appropriate offices. One more time I tried to catch sight of Said to say goodbye in sign language, and in the trick of windows and doors reflecting each other he briefly materialized as I passed a corridor leading to a gate. There he sat, his head cupped by a hand, staring out at the airfield. Then an opened door, or a window, or a shifting of surfaces ripped away the reflection and he was gone.

I walked to the rank of taxis with the unsteady stagger of an untouchable. Crumpled in my pocket was enough money to get me back to my hotel. One by one the drivers fell silent and walked away from me. I slowly got into the first car, told the driver my destination and how much I would pay him for the ride, and to his credit he nodded and put his foot on the accelerator.

The drive back into Algiers was memorable because it existed on a level only encountered in nightmares while fighting one's way to the surface. I saw very clearly the straight runway ahead as I watched from some cosmic eye the plane taking Said out of Algeria; the plane gaining momentum, lifting slowly into the air. His leaving took the place of mine. An eye for an eye. The driver said angrily, "It's the Oasis you wanted, isn't it? You're here." I paid him and got out; my key was handed to me with a yawn, I went up the staircase and let myself into my room. Naturally the passport and money were where I had left them, when I went back to get the bottle of scotch.

Chapter Nine

TUNISIA

Crouched next to the impoverished shadows, crouched next to dead trees still standing in lifeless fields, is a bedouin, or a small animal, or a bird. Even this will serve: a white stone kilometer marker with its square foot of shade offering the promise of shelter from the fierce sun of midday. There is no breeze, anywhere, that cools. The idea of *"cool"* is a useless abstraction, like walking, to someone with no limbs. When you drive along the deserted roads of southern Tunisia it seems as though you are actually flying in an envelope of heat, even though you know in a passing moment of logic that the wheels of the car are contacting the asphalt underneath. Perhaps, then, you are on a runway, the longest runway in North Africa, flanked on either side by some undefinable terrain that is neither desert nor earth nor seabed. Ahead and behind, the runway shimmers, lifts into space, breaks into pool-like reflections of water at the horizons. There is no difference between where you have been, where you are and where you are going. You will take off. You will fly. Not a soul will witness the event as you lift off the runway towards the mighty, all-powerful sun to be incinerated high above, your ashes scattering across this lost place.

You cannot forget the sun here; you must not forget it, for it is the key to the Arab world. Nothing can resist the force of the heat against the parched land. *Light upon light*, is written in the Koran, *Allah guides to his light whom he will*. It was a desert people who subscribed to Islam, a people long used to being magnetized by the fiery shield that rose each day in the sky. In discarding the Roman Church, they dedicated themselves to a religion that required a surrendering of self, totally, to a higher will.

Soon you will pass a crumbling village, its half-walls flanking the road. Depending on the angle of the sun, all the idle villagers will move in mass from one side of the highway to the other to hug the shadows there. When its inhabitants cross, the whole village seems to tilt with that motion, a wrecked raft drifting on that dry, useless sea. By now the plateau looks as though the lowest of tides has pulled back to some point on the distant horizon preparing for a colossal wave. You try to clear from your mind this succession of surreal images. After all, you must be responsible, *you are driving a car*. And then, with no warning, you have realized that the heat has become almost bearable. You have begun to breathe and swallow without thinking about it and without thinking about your thirst. You consult your map, you note the kilometer markers whose shadows have lengthened and paled. Figures on the landscape begin to move. A camel caravan turns its collective head to watch you speed by; there are tents with bedouins emerging from behind the flaps. From nowhere, a dog, readying its bark, comes rushing across a field to begin a losing race with you. Insects dash against your windshield. Ahead, way ahead, the jagged outline on both sides of the road gradually assumes the gentle, graceful shape of a palm grove. There will be a town before dark.

But that is in the south, and we will return there presently. In the north of Tunisia, things are different. The city of Tunis is extremely civilized. There is something blameless about Tunis, blameless, even bland. Gone is the suppressed rage of Algiers, the voracity of Casablanca. It is easier here, cleaner, gentler. Tunis is the San Francisco of North Africa. Its mechanisms run well. Traffic is regulated along the boulevards where policemen stand on display at the most popular intersections. They are white-gloved and theatrical. In California they would have sought jobs in the movies. After ten in the evening, honking is forbidden. Motorized wedding processions try to get through town before the clock strikes, before the white-gloved policemen hand out summonses. Traffic violations are dealt with in an organized fashion. I learned this when I was given a ticket. The policeman stopped me with an elegant salute. I asked whether he needed help in filling out the ticket from the information on my passport. He replied that certainly he did not, that his reading of English was probably equal to my reading of Arabic. As it turned out, he was right. We smiled, he saluted and went on his way. I glanced at the ticket before putting it in the glove compartment. I was written down as inhabiting a city called Green. I pondered this as I drove away, remembering, as I went through a stop sign, that it was my passport listing under "Eyes."

In bars that are not patronized by foreigners, they do not serve alcohol after eight to avoid drunken fights. They are all sensible rules set down by one of the most sensible rulers of our time. Throughout the small country—with less than six million people—he is known with affection as Habib. His photograph is everywhere. He has been in power since 1957, and so the pub-

lic has seen him age on their walls like a member of its family. It is a small enough family, and he has seen to it that it has begun to prosper. Factories under European financing have sprouted in Tunisia. Customs duties for their exports have been abolished. Tunisians now remain in Tunisia and no longer go off to Europe to get jobs. Political restrictions are less apparent here than elsewhere in the Arab world. Tunis might easily have been placed on the European coast of the Mediterranean. It is the only city in North Africa in which the following dialogue could have taken place. A street vendor had been trying to sell something to a tourist who had no interest in what was being sold.

"I'm sorry," said the tourist finally, "I really don't want it."

"Yes, yes. Of course," said the vendor. "You don't have to take it. This is a free country. Freedom is the most precious thing in the world. *Vive la liberté!*"

White-robed gentlemen in Tunis, some of them elderly, some of them

with thick spectacles, work with great precision on arranging jasmine blossoms into tiny bouquets. The flowers are threaded together and set into
sticks. They serve no other function than to give sensual pleasure. These jasmine sticks are held, twirled, fingered the way Greeks use worry beads, or
they are stuck behind the ears like a clerk's pencils. The gentlemen creating
these perfumed ornaments also string the blossoms together into necklaces.
Beginning at dusk, they are sold by strolling vendors who leave a trail of fra-
grance in their wake. There is no way to resist the jasmine. They cost almost
nothing. For a few cents you can weave a garden around you. Obediently
they send out their perfume, gradually darkening, exhausted by the flagrant
process of seduction. They are abandoned on café tables, left on automobile
seats, tossed onto night tables and pillows. In the morning, they have only
an acrid remembrance of their evening scent, the petals have shriveled and
hardened and they are thrown out.

> I also sought in vain that dark café where the only habitués were tall Negroes
> from the Sudan. Some of them had their big toe cut as a sign of slavery. Most
> of them wore, stuck in their turban, a little sprig of white flowers, of fragrant
> jasmine, which intoxicates them; it falls along the cheek like a curl of the roman-
> tic epoch and gives their face an expression of voluptuous languor. They like
> the odor of flowers to such an extent that often, not able to smell them strongly
> enough, they insert the crushed petals into their nostrils. In that café one of
> them would sing, another would tell stories, and tame doves would fly about and
> perch on their shoulders.*

It is tempting, often, to think that things were better before we got to
them; tempting to light on Gide's 1886 images of languor and doves and
glaze over the other image of slavery. To a traveler the past in the Arab
world takes on an enchantment because each separate element in it was
given a larger space in which to move, and the motion itself was more meas-
ured. Listen to a description of Hammamet in an 1895 guidebook: "A small
town of 3700 inhabitants, surrounded by a dilapidated wall and protected
by a citadel, clearly of Arab construction. The land in the neighborhood is
well watered, though sandy, and the place once did a considerable trade in
lemons, which were sent to Palermo for exportation to America."

Now, in Hammamet, busloads arrive, chartered planes, cars with foreign
plates, groups wearing name cards, tour leaders with whistles: their destination is the beaches of Tunisia. The country used to export flowers, olives,
fruit, wheat and wine. It had no oil, no minerals, no coal, no gas, twenty-

* The Journals of André Gide (1886: Tunis, February–March 1886) translated by
Justin O'Brien (New York: Alfred A. Knopf, 1947). Used by permission of Alfred A.
Knopf.

two kinds of poisonous snakes and four kinds of scorpions. And then it discovered that it had a salable coastline.

Everything is booked solid for the summer. The hotel lobbies are crammed full with incoming and outgoing luggage corralled like herds of petrified animals. Desk clerks cope with the colloidal mass of nationalities, the astonishing shapes and sizes and colors of the extraterritorial beings besieging them over their counters, their keys, their registers. In the hotel restaurants, dumbfounded Tunisian waiters try to keep up with the pace, try to carry, serve, pour, lift, balance and glide through the swinging doorways to the kitchen without a mishap. But unsuccessful journeys punctuate the meal as trays full of dishes fall crashing to the floor. All the waiters stop what they are doing to rush to the scene. The careful, regimented teachings of the Westernized hotel administration fly out of the neo-Moorish windows. Shouts from the kitchen volley across the ceilings. Everything is chaos. For that instant of time, the staff releases itself from all the imposed restrictions to be at last what it was once, before the coming of the vacationer to these lands, when the town was surrounded by a dilapidated wall and the neighborhood was well watered though sandy: village people rushing down the road to see what's happening.

Visiting the resorts in Tunisia is like watching a face smiling broadly when you know the brain is vacant. The atmosphere has not evolved. It is a Technicolor world imposed upon a monotone reality. The invasion of foreigners means new jobs, and money, and new aspirations, and no one has the spare time to wonder about it.

The last time I was in Hammamet, I found—at the end of the line—a slightly down-at-the-heels place, the variety that usually appeals to me. Small cottages needing repair were set along a pathway leading to the main building covered with vines. On the beach I sat under a faded umbrella with rusted spokes, and next to me, under an umbrella identical to mine, reclined an extraordinarily attractive blond couple whose even blonder child sat in front of them with a brightly colored sand pail and a tiny shovel. I propped a book on my knees and tried to read, but it was no good. Everywhere there were families, and couples, and ideal children playing. And, as a kind of backdrop, Tunisians in robes billowed along the seafront: proud galleons, those women; boats bobbed up and down with small Tunisian flags—it was a holiday—and nearby, in an area that was connected with the hotel, some women were thrashing sheep's hides in a shallow stream leading inland from the sea. Then they hung them up to dry in the sun as it quickly gained in the sky.

My blond neighbors conversed quietly in a Scandinavian language; then they got up to go in swimming together. Just before sprinting off to the water, the husband came over to me to ask me in perfect English—observing with a quick glance the language of the book I was reading, or trying to read—whether I might keep an eye on the child for a moment. I said that I certainly would, further retreating into the role of solitary gentleman surrounded on the seashore by a perfect day and other people's happiness.

The child, with his great blue eyes, was content to have me help him with his sand pail and looked on with interest as I tried to construct something resembling a small castle. Soon, his parents returned glistening and laughing from the sea.

"You've found a friend!" the mother said, adding to my discomfort. She shook her hair luxuriously in the sun and fell on the beach next to the child —unconcerned with getting her legs and elbows coated with sand—to smooth his hair away from his forehead. The husband, patting himself with a towel, made the introductions. Their name was Hansen.

I got to know the Hansens fairly well—their outlines, that is, for it seemed that wherever I was, whether it was taking a walk through the boutique-strewn town, or sitting in the hotel's dining room, they were there as well. I suppose you could say that we had the same rhythm, and I had the uneasy sensation that they were put into my path by some divine brochure maker to illustrate in living color what the mighty resort business was all about.

In any case, I was relieved to be asked to lunch at the villa of some acquaintances if only to remove myself from constant proximity to all the cozy families around me, the Hansens in particular. My hosts—I will call them Sahli—sent a driver to pick me up who then deposited me within the gardens of a house hidden from view and I found my way to a vast, cool, high-domed living room where I sat on a sofa and waited, as a clock ticked from some other room, for an hour. Finally I asked the servant who appeared noiselessly with a large glass of welcome lemonade how I would find a taxi to get me out of there. He muttered and shrugged, put on a pair of very old eyeglasses, consulted a telephone directory—moving his lips as he turned the pages—shut the directory and left with it. I wandered around the room, took art books down from high shelves, and found myself extremely disagreeable when my small hostess sauntered into the room from the doors leading to the terrace.

"Tunisian time!" she chirped. "Everyone is divinely late in this part of the world."

"Divine to you," I said ungallantly, "rude to me."

"But I've been mounting a *show!*" she said. "And you must come to the vernissage! Everyone will be there. Now don't be in such a foul temper. Adjust, when you're with Tunisians, to their schedule." And with that, she ran her hand across my brow and drifted out of the room.

Sahli, the husband, then appeared. He went straight to politics, waving away the offered lemonade.

"Strong leaders make strong countries," he said. "Habib is strong. He

isn't just photographed opening a school. Twenty-five percent of our budget goes into education. I bet you don't even have that in America. The number of children in school is three times what it was when we were occupied by the French."

The bespectacled servant advanced towards me with the telephone directory, his finger holding a page open.

"What's that?" asked Sahli.

"The number for the taxi," he answered.

"Where are you going?"

"Forget it," I said. "No, it's okay," I added to the servant, who was trying to hand me the opened book. If I was going to participate in a farce, I thought, I certainly had the materials.

"Bourguiba publicly drank *orange juice* during the *fasting* of Ramadan when he made a speech. *During Ramadan!* He wants to break tradition to strengthen the country." Sahli's skin, I noted, was the color people strive for in Beverly Hills.

"We have often dined with his son. He is very attractive," said pert Mme. Sahli as she returned, now in a yellow kaftan, looking extremely pretty. "Lunch, lunch, lunch!" she announced, and we followed her out onto the patio.

The garden was bright with the ravishing colors of bougainvillea and hibiscus. In the shade of the patio the air was still. There was the gratifying sound of ice against the ever-present glasses of lemonade.

"The land value practically doubles each year," said Mme. Sahli. "I'm awfully glad we built this place when we did." Her nostrils quivered with a kind of voluptuousness, an involuntary spasm I have seen on the faces of many acquisitive people.

"Everyone comes here now, builds houses, goes to the hotels," said the husband, embracing the landscape. "We have art galleries. It's like the Riviera, or like Capri."

I thought with longing of those two places in late September, when they are at their most beautiful, and I sighed involuntarily with certain happy memories.

"Ah, listen to Richard sigh," said the wife playfully. "You can see that he adores Hammamet. Here," she said portentously, "you will fall in love. Everyone does. No one's alone."

"No one's fool enough to *come* here alone," I said.

"This is a gentle country," said Sahli.

I agreed. I watched some small bright-colored birds circle the perfect corolla of a white hibiscus shot with deep red at its center. A large bowl of couscous was set down without a sound, the servant standing back in the shadows. The wife served us, talking amiably about how all the women who

meet her husband fall immediately in love with him, and he beamed indul-
gently, helping himself to the wonderful food. We seemed, at that table on
that patio in that garden, to have moved into that genteel parenthesis of
the international good life whose boundaries had nothing to do with nationalities. It is a movable feast, this parenthesis, floating in the distance just
outside the reach of almost everybody in the world.

"You're not at a good hotel," said the husband. "There is a fine hotel just
near here. I can arrange everything. The manager is a friend."

"Everyone is his friend," the wife teased. "You will love it. Come by tomorrow on our way to the vernissage. We'll take you there. With a pool, on
the sea, *beautiful* people." She fluttered her hands at the abundance. "Everything!"

I said that I would. We fixed a time and I made a mental note to take my
own car.

At dinner, the Hansens again took the table next to mine, smiling, each
of them wearing white. We asked each other how we had spent the afternoon and told each other how pleasant it sounded and then I looked fixedly
out of the window at the sea so that they could go back to talking to each
other, which they did immediately. It seemed to be an amorous conversation: seemed so, I say, because their lips would remain partly open at the
end of their phrases, and they stared carefully into each other's eyes, and I
read this as amorous. But I must admit that I had begun to forget exactly
what amorous was.

I went to bed early. On my first night there, I discovered and tried to
forget that the cottages were built in just such a way that blocked any breeze.
But by the second night, I could not avoid noticing that the air stopped
circulating at my windows, which admitted, instead, regiments of mosquitoes
rising from the sewage canal running nearby. The discotheque, set into the
hotel's courtyard, resound until three—I kept looking at my watch in an
effort to urge the night on—beamed to the stars sixties' rock music above, to
Orion and Cassiopeia and the rest of the constellations slowly moving across
the brilliant African sky. Finally I got dressed and went down in the dark to
the beach.

There was barely a moon, and just enough pale light silhouetted the
closed umbrellas. The fresh breeze coming from the sea clicked the metal
tips against the wooden posts, sounding like halyards in a boat dock. In the
careful row, one umbrella was open, on its side, like something fallen in a
platoon. In its shelter and its privacy, under a shawl, reclined my blond
neighbors. I felt a twinge of what I would like to believe was benevolence,
quickly followed by an intense irritation. It seemed inappropriate to be con-
fronted by this perfect pair wherever I went. As I turned away, I felt my
body tense, and in my surprise I almost laughed, to mock them, to mock

myself. I had been wrong after all. I walked quickly in the other direction. Under the shawl Hansen lay with a dark-haired figure whom I could not distinguish.

The next morning the Hansens were gone. Their faded umbrella was opened, their chairs were out, even the sand pail was there, but they never came. Into this vacant space, a local Tunisian wandered, hesitated, then sat; first one Tunisian, then another, and then another came by. One of them began playing with the child's pail, putting it on his head like a fez, to the general amusement of the others. Gradually they relaxed under the umbrella and the territory became theirs.

I drove to the villa an hour after the appointed time and was told by one of their staff that Monsieur and Madame had gone out separately, could I come back in an hour? I said that I could not, and set out to look for the hotel on my own. I found it, and it was closed and empty.

A young Tunisian was standing on the sidewalk in front of the apparently abandoned building trying to sell a fake Roman statue to a pretty French girl. I began to ask him what had happened to the hotel, but he was too engrossed in discussing the merits of the artifact to be disturbed. At one moment, with great agitation, he briefly put his hands on the shoulder of the girl and she seemed not to notice it as she named a lower price. And as he held her, his arms trembled, he became speechless and forgot his sales pitch. The statue, which he had been holding in the crook of his arm, slid, the girl caught it and giggled and I went up the hotel steps. *You will fall in love*, I thought wryly, *everybody does*.

I walked past an empty pool. Leaves slid along its turquoise tiles and a lizard scuttled down the children's steps. Near the diving board there were several mattresses, their foam-rubber innards protruding through the once bright, once red surfaces. I found a door to the lobby.

"Hello," I called. No one answered. It was now late afternoon and part of the vast room was in darkness. Chairs were stacked to the arched ceiling; I walked over to the front desk, the cloth across it sheathing the wood panels underneath. An elegant pier glass of a French design observed my solitary meandering, all the crowds and crush of another time no longer available to its reflections.

"*Fermé!*" said a guardian, coming in from another room.

"Why?" I asked. "What happened?"

"Already three months," he said. Then he moved his index finger and thumb together in the universal sign for money. "*Kaput, fineesh, finito*," he added, using several obligatory languages of the area.

I nodded. In the shadows I saw a piano, and I went over to it.

"No one plays," said the guard. "No one ever played. They brought it down here because it looked . . ." He looked to the ceiling for the word. "*Classique*."

I lifted the cover of the keyboard. It was a Pleyel, from Paris.
I touched one note and then another. The tune wobbled unsteadily.

> *No matter what price is paid*
> *What stars may fade*
> *Above*
> *I'll follow . . .*

"That is not the right music for here," the guard said abruptly. "You should play Arab music! This isn't Europe!"

I said that he was probably right, and I went out of the hotel, down the steps, into my car, and the next day I left Hammamet.

Kairouan—from caravan—is considered by Moslems the holiest city in North Africa. A series of visits to it, seven or so, compensate for a pilgrimage to Mecca. The town was created as a military fortress halfway, in the vast region between Morocco and Egypt, by Oqba ibn-Nafeh in 670, thirty-eight years after the death of Mohammed. It was supposed to have been infested with wild beasts and noxious animals. Ibn-Khaldun, the most respected historian in all Islam, wrote in the fourteenth century that Oqba gathered his army together and shouted to the trembling prairie, "Serpents and savage beasts, we are the companions of the blessed Prophet. Retire! We intend to establish ourselves here." The wild beasts withdrew, resulting in several immediate converts among the neighboring Berbers. When Tunis was occupied in 1883, the Holy City was attacked. Three different corps were dispatched to Kairouan, expecting a massive resistance. No Nazarene—Christian—had ever set foot behind the walls of the town. And once again, the French troops, commanded by General Etienne, marched through the open gates unopposed. There is no report on his precise actions and reactions once inside the space that had remained secluded for twelve hundred years.

Although Paul Klee is supposed to have found, in 1913, the colors in Kairouan that he would use in his pictures, the atmosphere of the Great Mosque is reminiscent of the early paintings of di Chirico. The immense, empty courtyard is paved in marble, bounded by long low walls, angled strangely, giving it a false perspective. The great minaret rises in diminishing quadrangles above, so restored over the ages that it has the atmosphere of something mummified, ominous. Roman stones have been incorporated into the buildings, some of them with ancient Latin inscriptions set upside down into the facings. Kufic writing in the Mosque tells of its early constructions during the reign of the Sanhaja Emirs in the year 1000, and the cypress beams go back a century before.

J'aime le karate, it says on the T-shirts. *The University of Chicago, Tulane, Harvard*, worn by the kids all over town. *D'accord, okay, ciao* are

thrown onto the heap of the internationalisms. *Let's get with it*, says someone urging a mule cart to let his car pass. You have to look hard, in this
holiest of cities, for the traditional greeting of the handshake followed by
the touching of the hand to the lips or heart. At dusk, the starlings circle
overhead; then they land chattering in the trees to bend the branches low,
obscuring the leaves.

The noise is like a shrieking crowd in a faraway arena. Up a flight of
dingy steps, there is a small room where a blindfolded camel will turn a
water wheel while a turbaned man waits for enough tourists to gather. "Zaa,"
he cries, and the camel stands with effort to begin a lumbering turn while
the mechanism drawing the well water groans and clanks. The water connects
to Mecca, says the man, passing the hat.

Along the road south a small child raises his arm, spreads his fingers
slowly in a salute; then he becomes a figure growing rapidly smaller in the
rearview mirror, watching the car disappear. In certain villages, everyone is
sour, as though some malaise had infected the territory. Young people band
together in a bitterness about not being elsewhere. Gathering near the local
gasoline station, they watch the cars speed by them, hoping that they will
stop. When the drivers and passengers get out, numbed from too much
time in the car, they stretch, sit exhausted in the local flyblown café, order
their coffees, which they consume with indifference, get back in their cars
and leave. Their disinterest does not pass unobserved, and day after day
it seeps into the kids gathering around the cars, into the gasoline attendant,
into the café waiter and, finally, into the town.

Some of the faces are so extraordinarily beautiful that they surpass all previous ideas—Western ideas, I suppose—of beauty, bringing them to another
uncharted level. A girl with a shawl, both of her hands busy, will hold an
edge of it between her teeth in an effort to hide her face, and the face, turning away solemnly, is a flawless combination of seduction and innocence.
The slender nape of a boy's neck will slowly turn to reveal a perfect profile;
a sudden regard through eyes framed by the thickest of lashes insinuates
something incomprehensible. Then it is gone. They are cat princesses and
fox princes and they dissolve into thin air if you wish to catch them.

Arriving in the larger rural towns is like approaching some terrestrial sub-
marine outfit. It is a world of men. The men are everywhere, lounging
against the walls, filling the squares, the café, the benches, crowding
through the streets, they are out doing business or passing the time of day.
In Europe, the only equivalent is in Sicily, where townfuls of men wearing
dark clothing and straw hats more somberly occupy the territory. Here, the
stranger is incorporated into the scene without surprise, as inevitable and
ephemeral as a bruise following a fall.

Women are glimpsed as they are in the rest of the Arab world, retreating
up stairs, down alleys; they close doors behind them, slip past windows,

draw back from roofs. When they are required to hasten through the streets, they reveal, beneath the thin wool of their long haiks, miniskirts of bright colors, blouses without sleeves, movie-star masks of cosmetics. The large country Berber ladies are less timid, trudging along all bangles and tattoos, jabbering like Gypsies, pale, wrinkled too young, their faces like forty miles of bad road.

There are lean terrible dogs foraging through the scant garbage. They look up, baring their teeth nervously, and they are so bewildered by kindness that it immobilizes them; then their ears lower, their tails wag with apology, they bow their heads with hope, their bodies now docile. The first sharp sound triggers their fearfulness and they slink away. The females lie heavily panting in the scraps of shadow, their eyes rueful, their undersides like bloated rubber gloves. Patiently they wait to expel the blind creatures inside them developing for their stark turn at the universe. And the cats are wraith thin, their ears unnaturally large, forever alert—in the paranoid way of cats more fortunate than they—for a calamity which in some way will implicate them.

Everyone is waiting. Everything is written down and God had determined it all from the beginning. *He is the Wise One, the All-knowing. He has knowledge of all that goes into the earth and all that springs up from it; all that comes down from heaven and all that ascends to it. He is the forgiving One, the Merciful.*

It was late in the afternoon, after the consuming sirocco had calmed. I had hired a horse-drawn carriage in the town of Gabès, where the oasis almost touches the sea. Beyond is an arid plateau, almost a desert, and when the heat is too strong, and threatens to scorch the earth, the bedouins come into the town seeking the breeze promised by the sea. The carriage tilted to receive me, its worn leathers and springs arthritic with creaks and groans.

"Is there time," I asked the coachman, "to go to the oasis before nightfall?"

"*Insh'Allah,*" he said, *if God wills it.*

He adjusted his battered fez, cracked his whip, and we set off, the horse laboring with effort, then beginning to trot as the whip snapped in the air. The carriage rolled diligently behind, wobbling unsteadily, although the canal alongside reflected back a smooth shadow gliding across it into a copse of trees. Now the oasis was revealed, opening itself, drawing our carriage into the narrow road between the palms, the fruit trees, the streams; somewhere there was a waterfall. Within the grove magical figures wove through shafts of late light, delicately traced. In the haze, women with jugs on their shoulders came into cloudy being, quivered, then disappeared as distant fountains splashed. Gates opened to long lanes where children came floating, bending under thick branches only to wash away among the grapevines. A stillness, a melting of the last rays of sun touched a horse raising its head, a lordly relative of our wretched animal now desperately trying to persevere, pulling the carriage in the oncoming darkness. We turned at the edge of the oasis and abruptly the illusion of richness and enchantment ended, cut clean through like stage scenery. These were the back streets of the town. The paths were clear; the houses down the lanes were half in ruins. There was no haze. Meager plantings stretched frail branches next to the earth, the leaves clawing the rubble. The canal alongside bubbled under a green slick of algae; a worn poster advertising toothpaste rusted upside down; children rushed around a corner to run after the carriage, trying to jump on its fender, and the coachman turned to crack his whip at them. They scattered, running still. An old man bent in half, carrying a weight of wood on his shoulders, skipped unevenly in front of us trying to hurry out of our way. The horse was urged on. People sat staring, squatted on the rotting doorsteps and on the ground. Down a side lane, a boy on crutches, his limp legs swinging, shouted, tilting his head forward with rage. The coachman's whip stung in the air.

"Easy," I said, my temper mounting, troubled about the animal and aware of some larger fear. "Take it easy with your whip."

"I'm going fast," said the coachman over his shoulder, "because there are no candles in the carriage lamps and it's already dark. I will get a ticket. I cannot afford a ticket."

We clattered along the streets, the horse picking up speed. On the sidewalk, people standing in front of dimly lit shopwindows glanced over at the sound of the wheels. Ahead, I saw a plump man sitting on a street corner with a candle burning in front of a typewriter, a scribe, listening to someone compose a letter. His eyeglasses glinted as he bent towards the keys; he stopped, looked around, began to call out, his hand shooting forward in alarm. Now the coachman was standing, his whip drawn back.

I lunged at him. "WHAT ARE YOU DOING?" I shouted, the dangerous part of my nature now in control of me. The wheel struck something, the carriage skidded noisily, leaned, righted itself. A boy sprawled near the curb, his arm flung across his face.

I had both shoulders of the man, shaking him. The carriage had stopped. The horse flicked its tail. From all corners, people came running.

"*Maktūb*" said the coachman, *it is written*, releasing himself from me with firm hands to step down into the street, to go to the boy.

With quick steps the scribe advanced towards me in the dark street as I jumped down from the carriage. He stopped, glanced at the boy in the gathering crowd and came over to me, polishing his lenses. In precise French he told me—hooking his eyeglasses onto his ears—that he had seen it all happen and that I needn't be upset, it was only a matter of a wounded leg, it happens here all the time. Then he stood back in his smudged robes, his pointed slippers together, to appraise me.

"It could have been prevented," I said gruffly, turning to go to the boy.

"Wait," he said, pattering after me. "Wait!" He stood now in front of me, thrusting his face up at mine.

"You are only a stranger to us," he said. "Here . . ." And he drew a circle with his stubby finger to indicate the crowd, the street and the imagined lands beyond. "If we thought about tomorrow, we would die!"

And at that moment, responding to him, the streetlamps flickered on, the scene was illuminated, frozen; then all was plunged in darkness as the lamps went off, and tried to light again.